ESPERANTO-ENGLISH
ENGLISH-ESPERANTO

DICTIONARY AND PHRASEBOOK

ABOUT THE AUTHOR

J.F. Conroy is the chairman of World Languages at a high school in Philadelphia, PA. He is the author of *Beginner's Esperanto* (Hippocrene), an introductory textbook for students of the International Language. Mr. Conroy has taught Esperanto at the high school and university levels, taking part in the annual Summer Esperanto Seminar at the University of Hartford, Connecticut.

ESPERANTO-ENGLISH
ENGLISH-ESPERANTO

DICTIONARY AND PHRASEBOOK

JOSEPH F. CONROY

HIPPOCRENE BOOKS, INC.
New York

ISBN 0-7818-0736-0

For information, address:
HIPPOCRENE BOOKS, INC.
171 Madison Avenue
New York, NY 10016

Printed in the United States of America.

CONTENTS
Enhavo

FOREWORD
Antaŭparolo

Esperanto is the language *that could*. If the people of the world decided to learn Esperanto as a universal second language, Esperanto could solve communication difficulties almost overnight. It could also save international businesses billions of dollars in translation costs. Esperanto could make learning a foreign language easier; once students mastered Esperanto, they would find learning national languages less daunting. As Esperantists have proved over and over again in the last one hundred years, Esperanto could do all of this easily and efficiently.

But Esperanto is also that language that *can*. It can open up a whole world of peoples and literatures to those who learn it. Esperanto can bring together people from the most distant parts of the earth and make them feel as though they really *are* part of one grand family. Today, right now, Esperanto is useful and worth learning. There are no foreigners in Esperanto-land!

Esperanto is arguably the most successful of constructed languages. In the more than one hundred years since L.L. Zamenhof created the language in Bialistok (Poland), Esperanto has grown tremendously while still remaining faithful to its original structure. A flourishing international literature awaits anyone who learns Esperanto, and the language has taken its place among the world's many tongues. The most recent statistics of the Universal Esperanto Association show active users of the language in 94 countries throughout the world from Albania to Zimbabwe.

Dr. Zamenhof entitled his first publication about Esperanto (1887) *Doktoro Esperanto: Lingvo Internacia*, "Doctor Hoping: International Language." *Esperanto* was not originally the name of the language, but the pseudonym Dr. Zamenhof used. But saying *la internacia lingvo de Doktoro Esperanto* was a bit long. This was soon shortened to just *Esperanto.*

This book you are holding in your hands was created in Esperanto and through Esperanto. In putting together the dictionary and phrasebook, I consulted with Esperantists around the world. My goal was to present the best international usage, avoiding anglicisms.

This dictionary and phrasebook is divided into four parts. The first presents the Esperanto alphabet and pronunciation. The second gives an overview of Esperanto grammar. The third part contains the Esperanto-English/English-Esperanto dictionary. The fourth and final part consists of set phrases and vocabulary for various topics; this is the phrasebook. At the end of the fourth part we have included some suggestions for further study, several Internet sites of interest, and a bibliography. There is also information on signing up for a free 10-lesson correspondence course offered by the Esperanto League for North America (ELNA) and the Canadian Esperanto Association (KEA).

To the many fellow Esperantists who so willingly offered their assistance in this project, I wish to express my deep gratitude and appreciation. *Multajn elkorajn dankojn!*

All of us in *Esperantio* ("the land where Esperanto is spoken," that is, the whole world) wish you well as you discover our remarkably rich language. *Bonan vojaĝon!*

PART ONE—THE ESPERANTO ALPHABET AND PRONUNCIATION
Unua Parto—La Aboco kaj la Prononco

The Esperanto alphabet consists of 28 letters. Each letter represents one sound, and each sound is represented by only one letter. There are no silent letters. These features make Esperanto easy to spell and easy to read.

The vowel letters are **a, e, i, o, u**. They are pronounced approximately as follows:

a - as "a" in *father*
e - as "e" in *met*, sometimes closer to "a" in *mate*
i - as "ee" in *meet*
o - as "oa" in *boat*
u - as "oo" in *hoot*

The letters **j** and **ŭ** function as semi-vowels. They help form diphthongs:

aj - as "igh" in *high*
oj - as "oy" in *toy*
uj - "oo" followed by a quick **i**-sound
aŭ - as "ow" in *how*
eŭ - "eh" followed by a quick **u**-sound

The consonant letters can be divided into three groups. The first group consists of those letters which are the same as letters of the English alphabet, and which have approximately the same sound:

b, d, f, h, k, m, n, p, t, v, z

The second group consists of those letters which are the same as letters of the English alphabet but which have a different sound:

c	- as "ts" in *cats*
g	- always hard as in *gun*, never as in *gem*
j	- as "y" in *yes*
l	- always as in *light*, never as in *milk*
r	- always trilled as in Spanish or Italian
s	- always as in *hiss*, never as in *rose*

The third group of consonants consists of those letters which have a circumflex (^) above them:

ĉ	- as "ch" in *chin*
ĝ	- as "g" in *gem*
ĥ	- as "ch" in *Bach*
ĵ	- as "z" in *azure*
ŝ	- as "sh" in *shoe*

Alphabetical order is as follows:

a b c ĉ d e f g ĝ h ĥ i j ĵ k l m n o p r s ŝ t u ŭ v z

Note that the letters **q, w, x,** and **y** are not part of the Esperanto alphabet. The name of each vowel is simply the sound of that letter. The name of each consonant is the sound of that letter followed by the vowel **o: a, bo, co, ĉo, do, e, fo**, etc.

Double consonants are rare in Esperanto. When they occur, this almost always signals a compound word. For example, *huffero*, "horseshoe," is a compound of *huf-o* ("hoof") and *fer-o* ("iron").

Every word of more than one syllable is accented on the next-to-the-last syllable: *Esperanto*, "ehs-peh-RAN-toh"; *familio*, "fah-mee-LEE-oh". Words of one syllable may be accented as needed.

PART TWO—AN OVERVIEW OF ESPERANTO GRAMMAR
Dua Parto—Mallonge Pri la Gramatiko

One of the unique features of Esperanto is that its grammar is relatively simple and free from annoying irregularities and most exceptions. Once you have learned a rule, you may depend upon applying it in every suitable situation.

At first sight, Esperanto may resemble familiar West-European languages, but underneath this similarity beats a mechanism far different from those tongues. Many linguists classify Esperanto as an *agglutinative* language, such as Turkish or Hungarian. To the invariable wordstock of noun, adjective and verb roots we add unchanging and well-defined prefixes and suffixes to derive further words. These prefixes and suffixes themselves may also occur as independent words, a situation quite different from that found in English, French or Spanish.

1. *The Noun*: In Esperanto, *every noun ends in* **-o** in the singular: *birdo, libro, sinjoro, samideano*. The plural adds **-j**: *birdoj, libroj, sinjoroj* (**-oj** sounds like **oy** in English "toy").

When the noun is the *direct object* of a verb or means "motion toward," it adds an **-n**: *birdon/birdojn, libron/librojn, sinjoron/sinjorojn*. The following sentences mean about the same thing; the **-n** helps us distinguish the direct object:

La kato manĝis la muson.
La muson la kato manĝis.
La kato la muson manĝis.
La muson manĝis la kato.   The cat ate the mouse.

The different word-order serves to emphasize different parts of the sentence.

By the way, there is only one word for "the," *la*. There is no word for "a/an"; just use the noun by itself: *libro*, "a book."

2. *The Adjective*: All adjectives end in **-a** in the singular: *bona, granda, ĉarma*. When used with plural nouns, the adjective also adds **-j**: *bonaj katoj, grandaj birdoj, ĉarmaj sinjorinoj* (**-aj** sounds like **y** in English "try").

When used with a direct object noun, the adjective also adds **-n**:

Mi konas la grandan sinjoron.

I know the big man.

Ni aĉetis la belajn bildojn.

We bought the beautiful pictures.

For "more" we use *pli*: *pli inteligenta*, "more intelligent." "Less" is *malpli*: *malpli multekosta*, "less expensive." We complete comparisons with *ol*, "than": *Esperanto estas pli facila ol la angla.* ("Esperanto is easier than English.")

Plej (sounds like English "play") is used for "most": *la plej grava urbo*, "the most important city." For "least," use *malplej*. We complete such sentences with *el*: *Mia kato estas la plej inteligenta el ĉiuj bestoj.* ("My cat is the most intelligent of all animals.")

In Esperanto, adjectives usually precede their noun, but they may just as well follow it: *bona hundo, hundo bona* ("a good dog").

By changing the final **-o** to **-a**, any noun can become an adjective.

3. *Pronouns*: Here are the basic pronouns used as *subjects* and as *objects of prepositions*:

singular		plural	
I	*mi*	we	*ni*
you	*vi*	you	*vi*
he	*li*	they	*ili*
she	*ŝi*		
it	*ĝi*		
one	*oni* ("people say, they say, etc.")		

Ŝi parolis kun ili en la vendejo.
She spoke with them in the store.

For "himself, herself, itself, themselves," there is one form, *si*.

For *direct objects*, we simple add the same **-n** as for nouns and adjectives:

singular		plural	
me	*min*	us	*nin*
you	*vin*	you	*vin*
him	*lin*	them	*ilin*
her	*ŝin*		
it	*ĝin*		

Ili ne vidas vin.	They don't see you.
Vi ne vidas ilin.	You don't see them.

The word *si* also takes an **-n**: *sin*.

To form possessive adjectives, we add **-a** to the base forms of the pronouns, just as we did for all other adjectives: *mi* > *mia*, "my." These forms can add **-j** for the plural (*miaj*) and **-n** for the direct object (*mian, miajn*).

singular		plural	
my	*mia*	our	*nia*
your	*via*	your	*via*
his	*lia*	their	*ilia*
her	*ŝia*		("ee-LEE-ah")
its	*ĝia*		

There is one further possessive form, *sia*. This refers to a third-person subject:

Petro telefonis sian fraton.

Peter called his (own) brother.

Petro telefonis lian fraton.

Peter called his (someone else's) brother.

4. *Verbs*: Unlike the situation in many languages, where the verb system is a horror, in Esperanto the forms are simple. There is only one set of endings, only one ending for each tense, and...*there are no exceptions!*

Infinitive (**-i**)	vidi	marŝi	esti
	"to see"	"to walk"	"to be"
Imperative (**-u**)	vidu	marŝu	estu
	"see!"	"walk!"	"be!"
Present (**-as**)	vidas	marŝas	estas
	"sees"	"walks"	"is, etc."
Past (**-is**)	vidis	marŝis	estis
	"saw"	"walked"	"was/were"
Future (**-os**)	vidos	marŝos	estos
	"will see"	"will walk"	"will be"
Conditional (**-us**)	vidus	marŝus	estus
	"would see"	"would walk"	"would be"

The negative uses *ne*.

Mi ne vidis lin, sed mi vidos lin.

"I didn't see him, but I shall see him."

Li ne estas preta nun, sed li estos preta.

"He is not ready now, but he will be ready."

There are six *participles* in Esperanto, and they are widely used. When they occur as part of a compound verb, participles behave just like adjectives

(**-a/-aj**). When they end in **-o**, they mean "person who...".

	active	passive
present	*kantanta*	*kantata*
past	*katinta*	*kantita*
future	*katonta*	*kantota*

Here are some examples with translations:

la kantota ario	the aria about to be sung
la kantonta knabino	the girl about to sing
la kantata ario	the aria (now) being sung
la kantanta knabino	the singing girl
la kantita ario	the aria which was sung
la kantinta knabino	the girl who sang
la vojaĝonto	the person who is going to travel
la vojaĝanto	the person who is traveling, the traveler
la vojaĝinto	the person who has traveled

Participles which refer to the subject of a sentence end in *-e*:

Vidinte la urbon, ni estis kontentaj.

("Having seen the city, we were happy.")

When looking up an Esperanto verb in the dictionary, it is important to note whether it is *transitive* (can have a direct object) or *intransitive* (does not have a direct object). To make a transitive verb intransitive, we use the suffix *-iĝ-*:

I close the door.	*Mi fermas la pordon.*
The door closes.	*La pordo fermiĝas.*

A second suffix, *-ig-*, serves to create causative verbs:

I close the door.	*Mi fermas la pordon.*
I have the door closed.	*Mi fermigas la pordon.*

The suffix *-ad-* names the action of the verb:

to hammer	*marteli*
a hammer	*martelo*
a hammering	*martelado*

Both *-et-* (diminutive) and *-eg-* (intensive) also occur with verbs:

to laugh	*ridi*
to snicker	*rideti*
to laugh uproariously	*ridegi*

5. *Adverbs*: Adverbs are widely used in Esperanto. They end in **-e**: *bone* ("well"), *rapide* ("quickly"), *malfeliĉe* ("unfortunately"). Used with the direct-object **-n**, adverbs take on the meaning of "toward, into": *norden* ("northward"), *maldekstren* (leftward, to the left"), *traduki Esperanten* ("translate into Esperanto").

There are also a few basic adverbs ending in **-aŭ**: *ankoraŭ* ("still"), *preskaŭ* ("almost"), *baldaŭ* ("soon"), and the like. These adverbs provide some variety in a sentence.

6. *Prepositions*: The meanings of Esperanto prepositions are more rigidly defined that those of many national languages. It is important to keep the basic meaning of the preposition in mind when deciding which one to use.

al	- to, toward
anstataŭ	- instead of
antaŭ	- before, in front of
apud	- near
ĉe	- at
ĉirkaŭ	- around
da	- (quantity) of
de	- of, from

dum	- during, while
ekster	- outside of
el	- out of, out from
en	- in
ĝis	- until
inter	- between, among
je	- indefinite meaning
kontraŭ	- against, opposite
krom	- besides
kun	- with (in the company of)
laŭ	- according to, along
malantaŭ	- behind, in back of
malgraŭ	- despite
per	- by means of
po	- at the rate of
por	- for, in order to
post	- after
preter	- beyond
pri	- concerning
pro	- because of, owing to
sen	- without
sub	- under, beneath
super	- above
sur	- on
tra	- through
trans	- across

Note: The preposition *je* is not rigorously defined; it can be used where no other preposition fits.

After prepositions, the *subject* form of nouns, pronouns and adjectives usually occurs:

with the girls	*kun la knabinoj*
without me	*sen mi*
under the big tree	*sub la granda arbo*

If we intend to emphasize *motion toward*, then we add the direct object ending **-n**:

The cat is jumping on the bed.
La kato saltas sur la lito.
The cat jumps *onto* the bed.
La kato saltas sur la liton.
We are running under the tree.
Ni kuras sub la arbo.
We are running (toward a place) under the tree.
Ni kuras sub la arbon.

7. *Affixes*: The use of affixes allows the Esperanto-speaker to create a large word-store from relatively few roots. Affixes may also appear as independent words.

Prefixes

bo-	- relative by marriage (in-law)
dis-	- separation
ek-	- beginning, suddenness
eks-	- former
ge-	- both sexes together
mal-	- directly opposite
mis-	- wrongly
pra-	- remoteness of relationship or time
re-	- return, repetition

Suffixes

-aĉ-	- disparagement
-ad-	- prolonged, repeated, habitual action
-aĵ-	- concrete manifestation of the root word, a thing: *belaĵo*, "a beautiful thing."
-an-	- member, inhabitant
-ar-	- collective, group
-ebl-	- possibility
-ec-	- abstract quality of root word: *beleco*, "beauty"

-eg-	- augmentative (makes bigger, more intense)
-ej-	- place for
-em-	- tendency
-end-	- obligation: what must be...ed
-er-	- small particle of a whole
-estr-	- leader
-et-	- diminutive (makes smaller, less intense)
-id-	- offspring, descendent
-ig-	- cause, make
-iĝ-	- become, get
-il-	- tool, instrument, means
-in-	- female
-ind-	- worthiness (worthy of being...ed)
-ing	- holder for one item, socket
-ism-	- system of belief
-ist-	- person habitually associated with...
-obl-	- multiple of a number
-on-	- fraction
-op-	- collective numeral
-uj-	- container for, receptacle
-ul-	- person
-um-	- no fixed meaning

Note: Like the preposition *je*, the suffix *-um-* has not been rigorously defined. It serves to derive words somehow related to the basic sense of a root.

Grammatical Suffixes

-a	- adjective
-ant-	- present active participle: *portanta*, "carrying"
-as	- present tense verb
-at-	- present passive participle: *portata*, "being carried"
-e	- adverb
-i	- infinitive of verb

-int-	- past active participle: *portinta*, "having carried"	
-is	- past tense verb	
-it-	- past passive participle: *portita*, "having been carried"	
-o	- noun	
-ont-	- future active participle: *portonta*, "about to carry"	
-os	- future tense verb	
-ot-	- future passive participle: *portota*, "about to be carried"	
-u	- imperative verb	
-us	- conditional verb	

8. *Word-building*

Unlike many languages, Esperanto allows and encourages word-building. Rather than memorize long lists of specific terms, the Esperanto speaker is often able to create the word needed on the spot. For example, if you forget that *reptilio* is the biological term for "reptile," you can always use *rampulo*, "something that crawls."

Compound words are also frequent in Esperanto. One famous family of compounds uses the word *tuko*, "cloth." We find:

bantuko	bath towel	(*bano*, "bath")
bebtuko	diaper	(*bebo*, "baby")
buŝtuko	napkin	(*buŝo*, "mouth")
lavtuko	washcloth	(*lavi*, "to wash")
littuko	bed sheet	(*lito*, "bed")
mantuko	hand towel	(*mano*, "hand")
mortotuko	shroud	(*morto*, "death")
naztuko	handkerchief	(*nazo*, "nose")
tablotuko	tablecloth	(*tablo*, "table")
viŝtuko	terry cloth	(*viŝi*, "to wipe")

Here are some words derived from the root *lern/i*, "to learn":

lerni   to learn
lernado   learning
lernanto   pupil
lernejo   school
lernolibro textbook

To make the most of Esperanto's unique structure, it is important to have a good working knowledge of the prefixes and suffixes in the language.

9. *Word-order*

Esperanto allows for a relatively free word order in sentences. Whether we say *Vin mi vidas* or *Mi vidas vin* ("I see you ...") is a matter of personal preference. Most often, we find the familiar English pattern of subject-verb-object (*La hundo kisas la knabinon*, "The dog kisses the girl."). Another popular pattern puts the direct object first: *La knabinon la hundo kisas*. The existence of the direct object ending *-n* always makes clear the subject and the object of a sentence.

PART THREE—THE DICTIONARY
Tria Parto—La Vortaro

ESPERANTO-ENGLISH DICTIONARY
Esperanto-Angla Vortaro

Words are listed by the nature of their roots. Noun roots have a final *-o*; verb roots, a final *-i*; adjective roots, a final *-a*. This will aid in deriving further words. For all adjectives and verbs, remember that the prefix *mal-* will provide you with a word which has the exact *opposite* meaning, e.g. *ferm-i*, "to open" will become *malferm-i*, "to close."

In this work we have followed the standard English system of alphabetizing. In Esperanto-language dictionaries, the final letters **-o, -a, -i** are often set off by a dash or a slash and do not count in alphabetizing. This means that in an Esperanto dictionary *arb/o* ("tree") will come before *arbar/o* ("forest"). In our present dictionary, *arbaro* will precede *arbo*.

A

abdomeno	abdomen
aboni	to subscribe
abono	subscription
abrikoto	apricot
aĉeti	to buy
adreso	address
aero	air
aeroporto	airport
afabla	kind, nice, pleasant

afero	affair, business, matter
aglo	eagle
aĝo	age
ajlo	garlic
ajn	at all
io ajn	anything at all
aĵo	thing, object
akademio	academy
akcipitro	hawk
akrido	grasshopper
aktiva	active
akto	act
aktoro	actor
akvo	water
alia	other
aliflanke	on the other hand
aligatoro	alligator
aliloka	elsewhere
alporti	to bring
alta	high
alumeto	match (for fire)
alveni	to arrive
ambaŭ	both
ambulanco	ambulance
amfibio	amphibian
ami	to love
amiko	friend
ananaso	pineapple
anaso	duck
anĉovo	anchovy
angilo	eel

angio	(blood) vessel
angla	English (language)
angle	in English
Anglio	England
Anglo	Englishman
ankoraŭ	still, yet
ano	member (of club, etc.)
ansero	goose
antaŭ	before
antaŭparolo	foreword
apartmento	apartment
aplaŭdi	to applaud
apoteko	pharmacy
araneaĵo	spiderweb
araneo	spider
arbaro	forest
arbo	tree
arĝento	silver
ario	aria
arko	arch
artiko	joint (anatomy)
asocio	association
asparago	asparagus
atendi	to wait
atenteme	attentively
atenti	to pay attention
atento	attention
aŭ	or
aŭdi	to hear
aŭdvida	video tape
magnetofono	recorder

aŭreolo	halo
aŭskulti	to listen
aŭto	auto, car
aŭtobuso	bus
avara	greedy
averto	warning
aviadilo	aircraft
avio	airplane
avo	grandfather

B

bakejo	bakery
baki	to bake
bakisto	baker
balai	to sweep
balailo	broom
baldaŭ	soon
baleno	whale
banano	banana
banko	bank
bano	bath
barbo	beard
barbulo	bearded man
basbalo	baseball (the sport)
basketbalo	basketball (the sport)
bastono	stick
batato	sweet potato
bazaro	market
bebo	baby
bebotuko	diaper

beko	beak
bela	beautiful
beleta	pretty
bendo	tape
benko	bench
besto	animal
bezoni	to need
biblioteko	library
biciklo	bicycle
bieno	farm
biero	beer
bifsteko	beefsteak
bildo	picture
bileto	ticket
birdo	bird
blanka	white
blato	roach
blonda	blond
blua	blue
bluzo	blouse
boato	boat
bobeno	reel, spool, bobbin
bona	good
bonkora	goodhearted
bonpreza	well-priced, bargain
bonveno	welcome
bonvolu	please be so kind as to
botelo	bottle
boto	boot
bovaĵo	beef (meat)
bovlo	bowl

bovo	ox, cow, bull, a bovine
brakhorloĝo	wristwatch
brako	arm
brasiko	cabbage
breco	pretzel
brila	bright, shining
brili	to shine
brokolo	broccoli
broso	brush
brovo	eyebrow
bruna	brown
brusto	chest (anatomy)
buĉi	to butcher
bufo	toad
bulko	roll (bread)
bunta	multi-colored
burgo	burger
buŝo	mouth
buŝtuko	napkin
butero	butter
butiko	store, shop

C

cedi	to yield
celebri	to celebrate
celerio	celery
celi	to have as a goal, to aim at
celo	goal
cemento	cement

cendo	cent (U.S. coin)
cent	one hundred
centra	central
centro	center
cenzuri	to censure
cepo	onion
cerbo	brain
certa	certain, sure
certe	certainly, surely
cervo	deer
cetera	the remaining
cidro	cider
cifero	figure, digit
cigaredo	cigarette
cigaro	cigar
cigno	swan
ciklo	cycle
cinamo	cinnamon
cirko	circus
citi	to quote, cite
citro	zither
citrono	lemon
civilizacio	civilization
colo	inch
cunamo	tsunami

Ĉ

ĉambro	room
ĉapelo	hat
ĉapo	cap

ĉar	because
ĉaro	cart
ĉasado	hunting
ĉasi	to hunt
ĉe	at
ĉeesti	to be present, attend
ĉefa	chief, main
ĉefurbo	capital city
ĉeko	(bank) check
ĉelo	cell
ĉemizo	shirt
ĉerizo	cherry
ĉevalo	horse
ĉia	every kind of
ĉial	for every reason
ĉiam	always, at every time
ĉie	everywhere
ĉiel	in every manner
ĉielo	sky
ĉies	everyone's
ĉio	everything
ĉiom	every quantity/amount
ĉiu	everyone
ĉokolado	chocolate
ĉu	question-word, turning a statement into a question

D

danĝero	danger
danki	to thank
dankinde	worthy of thanks
dato	date
de	of, from
debeto	debit
deca	fitting, proper
dekstra	right (not left)
delegito	delegate
demandi	to ask
demando	question
demeti	to lay (eggs)
denove	again
dentisto	dentist
dento	tooth
dentomedicino	dentistry
deserto	dessert
deveni	to come from
devi	to be obliged to
dezerto	desert
deziri	to desire
diable	devilishly, very
diablo	devil
diino	goddess
dio	god
direkta	direct, straightforward
direktoro	director
diri	to say
disko	disk, disc

disponi	to have available
distanco	distance
disvastigi	to spread (news, illness)
diversa	diverse
do	thus, therefore
doganisto	customs officer
dogano	customs (border)
dolaro	dollar
dolori	to hurt
dolorigi	to cause hurt to
doloro	pain
domo	house
donaco	gift
doni	to give
dormi	to sleep
dormoĉambro	bedroom
dorso	back
dorsosako	backpack
dosiero	file
dubi	to doubt
dubo	doubt
dum	while, during
duŝo	shower

E

eble	perhaps, maybe
ebria	drunk, inebriated
eĉ (Eĉ mi komprenas!)	even (Even *I* understand!)
edziĝi	to get married

edzo	husband
ek	sudden action
ekde	since
eksiĝi	to retire
eksmoda	out of fashion
ekzisti	to exist
elefanto	elephant
eleganta	elegant
elekti	to choose
elektriko	electricity
elirejo	exit
eliri	to go out
elitiĝi	to get out of bed
elkora	heartfelt
elŝuti	to download
enhavo	contents
enirejo	entrance
eniri	to enter
enkonduki	to introduce (a topic)
enlitiĝi	to go to bed
entuziasmo	enthusiasm
episkopo	bishop
epoko	epoch
esperi	to hope
estaĵo	being, creature
esti	to be
estimi	to value, esteem
estro	leader
etaĝo	floor (of a building)
Eŭropo	Europe

F

fabelo	fairy-tale
fablo	fable
fabo	broad bean
fabriko	factory
facila	easy
fajro	fire
fakte	in fact
fali	to fall
fama	famous
familio	family
fantomo	ghost
fari	to do, make
farti	to fare
fazeolo	string bean
febro	fever
feliĉe	happily, fortunately
fenestro	window
ferio	holiday
fermi	to close
fero	iron (metal)
fervoro	zeal
festo	festival
fiera	proud
fiero	pride
filmo	film
filo	son
fingro	finger
fini	to finish (something)
finiĝi	to come to an end

fiŝkapti	to go fishing
fiŝo	fish
flago	flag
flava	yellow
flegi	to nurse in sickness
flegistino	nurse
fleso	flounder (fish)
floko	flake
florbrasiko	cauliflower
floro	flower
flughaveno	airport
flugi	to fly
flugilo	a wing
foje	at one time, sometimes
fojo	time, occasion
foko	seal (animal)
for	away
fordoni	to give away
forgesi	to forget
foriri	to go away, leave
forko	fork
formiko	ant
forno	oven
fotelo	armchair
frago	strawberry
franca	French (language, etc.)
france	in French
Francio	France
Franco	Frenchman
frankfurto	hot dog
frato	brother

fraŭlino	Miss, young lady
fraŭlo	unmarried man
frazo	sentence
fremda	foreign
frida	cold
fridujo	refrigerator
fromaĝo	cheese
frosti	to freeze
frua	early
frukto	fruit
fulmo	lightening
fumi	to smoke
fundamenta	fundamental
funkcii	to function
futbalo	soccer

G

gaja	happy, joyful
galaksio	galaxy
galerio	gallery
galoŝoj	galoshes, overshoes
gangstero	gangster
ganto	glove
garaĝo	garage (for repairs)
garantio	guarantee
gaso	gas
gasto	guest
gaŭĝo	gauge
gazeto	magazine
gazono	lawn

generalo	general (military rank)
geno	gene
genuo	knee
giĉeto	ticket window
glaciaĵo	ice cream
glaciiĝi	to turn to ice
glacikubo	ice cube
glacio	ice
glaciteo	iced tea
gladi	to iron
gladilo	an iron
glaso	glass
glavo	sword
gliti	to slide
glitŝuo	skate
glubendo	adhesive tape
gluo	glue
gluteo	buttock, rump
golo	goal (sports)
gorĝo	throat
gorilo	gorilla
grado	degree
gramatiko	grammar
gramo	gram (metric)
granda	big
grapfrukto	grapefruit
gratuli	to congratulate
gratulo	congratulations
grava	important, grave
gravi	to matter, be important
ne gravas	it doesn't matter

gripo	flu
griza	gray
gusti	to taste like
gusto	the taste (of something)
gustumi	to taste something
guto	drop (of liquid)
gvidi	to guide

Ĝ

ĝangalo	jungle
ĝardeno	garden
ĝemelo	twin
ĝemi	to groan
ĝenerala	general (not specific)
ĝeni	to disturb
ĝentila	polite
ĝi	it
ĝia	its
ĝin	it (as direct object)
ĝinzo	blue jeans
ĝis	until
ĝis revido	see you again
ĝojo	joy
ĝui	to enjoy
ĝusta	exact

H

haro	hair; a (strand) of hair
haŭto	skin
havi	to have
hejme	at home
hejmen	homeward
hejmo	home
hela	light (in color)
helikoko	snail
helpi	to help
hepato	liver
hipogloso	halibut (fish)
hirundo	swallow (bird)
hispana	Spanish
hispane	in Spanish
Hispanio	Spain
Hispano	Spaniard
historio	history
hodiaŭ	today
homaro	mankind
homo	human being
horloĝo	clock
horo	hour
hospitalo	hospital
hotelo	hotel
hufo	hoof
huffero	horseshoe
hundo	dog

Ĥ

Note: The letter **ĥ** is rare in Esperanto. Words once spelled with **ĥ** have often been rewritten with either **ĉ** or **k**: *ĥino* ("Chinese") > *Ĉino*; *ĥemio* ("chemistry") > *kemio*.

ĥaoso	chaos
ĥolero	cholera
ĥoralo	chorale
ĥoro	choir

I

ia	some kind of
ial	for some reason
iam	sometime
ideo	idea
ido	offspring
ie	somewhere
iel	somehow
ies	someone's
iksodo	tick (insect)
ili	they
ilia	their
ilin	them
ilo	instrument
imamo	imam
infano	child
inĝeniero	engineer
inkluzivi	to include

insekto	insect
insigno	sign
instali	to install
instrui	to teach
instruisto	teacher
inteligenta	intelligent
intenci	to intend
interesa	interesting
io	something
iom	some quantity
iomete	a little bit
iu	someone

J

ja	indeed
jako	jacket
jam	already
Japana	Japanese
japane	in Japanese
Japanio	Japan
Japano	Japanese man
jarcento	century
jardeko	decade
jarlibro	yearbook
jarmilo	millennium
jaro	year
jen	behold, here's...
jes	yes
juna	young

junulo	young person
jupo	skirt

ĵ

ĵaluza	jealous
ĵargono	jargon
ĵazo	jazz
ĵeleo	jelly
ĵeti	to throw
ĵetono	token
ĵipo	jeep
ĵongli	to juggle
ĵudo	judo
ĵuri	to take an oath
ĵurnalo	newspaper
ĵus	just a moment ago

K

kaĉo	cooked cereal, mush
kafejo	café, coffee shop
kafo	coffee
kaj	and
kajenkolbaso	pepperoni
kajero	notebook
kalkano	heel (of foot)
kalkuli	to calculate
kalkulo	bill (restaurant)
kalsoneto	underpants, panties
kamiono	truck

Kanada	Canadian
Kanadano	Canadian citizen
Kanado	Canada
kanapo	couch
kandelo	candle
kanti	to sing
kanto	song
kapo	head
kapro	goat
kapti	to catch
karoto	carrot
karto	card
karuselo	carousel
kaskedo	cap
katedralo	cathedral
kato	cat
kateno	shackles
keĉupo	ketchup
kelka	some
kelnero	waiter
kesto	chest, case (box)
kia	what kind of
kial	why
kiam	when
kie	where
kiel	how, in what way
kies	whose
kikero	garbanzo, chick-pea
kilogramo	kilogram
kilometro	kilometer
kinejo	movie house

kio	what
kiom	how much/many
kisi	to kiss
kiu	who, which
klabo	bat (baseball, etc.)
klapo	flap, valve
knabo	boy
knedi	to knead
kodo	code
kokaĵo	chicken (meat)
koko	chicken
kokcinelo	ladybird beetle
kolbaso	sausage
kolego	colleague
kolo	neck
koloro	color
komenci	to begin
komercisto	merchant, businessman
komerco	business
kompakta	compact
kompreneble	understandably
kompreni	to understand
komputoro	computer
koni	to know someone
konsenti	to agree
konstelacio	constellation
konto	account
kontoro	office
korbo	basket
korespondi	to correspond
koro	heart

korpo	body
korto	courtyard
korvo	crow
kosmetikejo	beauty shop
kosti	to cost
kotono	cotton
koverto	envelope
krabo	crab
kredi	to believe
kredito	credit
krei	to create
kremo	cream
kringo	bagel
krokodilo	crocodile
kruro	leg
kubuto	elbow
kuirejo	kitchen
kuiri	to cook
kuko	cake
kukumo	cucumber
kulero	spoon
kultivi	to cultivate, farm
kun	with
kuniklo	rabbit
kunsido	meeting
kuraci	to cure
kuracisto	physician
kuraĝo	courage
kuseno	cushion, pillow
kutime	usually
kuvo	tub

| kuzo | cousin |
| kvadrata | square |

L

la	the
labori	to work
laboristo	worker
lacerto	lizard
lago	lake
lakto	milk
laktuko	lettuce
lampo	lamp
lando	land, country
lango	tongue (anatomy)
larĝa	wide
laŭdi	to praise
laŭmoda	fashionable, in style
lavejo	washroom
lavi	to wash
lavujo	washbasin
legi	to read
legomo	vegetable
leono	lion
leporo	hare (animal)
lernanto	student
lernejo ·	school
lerni	to learn
lernolibro	textbook
letero	letter (to send)
levi	to lift

leviĝi	to get up
li	he
lia	his
libera	free (not occupied)
libertempo	free time
libro	book
liceo	high school
lifto	elevator
limonado	lemonade
lin	him
lingvo	language
lipharoj	mustache
lipo	lip
listo	list
litero	letter (alphabet)
lito	bed
litro	liter (metric)
littuko	(bed) sheet
loĝi	to dwell, live somewhere
loko	place
lokusto	locust (insect)
longa	long
ludi	to play
ludilo	toy
lui	to rent
lumo	light
lunĉo	lunch
luno	moon
lupfantomo	werewolf
lupo	wolf

M

majonezo	mayonnaise
magnetofono	tape recorder
mal-	opposite of root meaning
maldekstra	left (left hand, left side)
male	just the opposite
maleolo	ankle
mallaŭdi	to condemn, scorn
malofte	rarely
malplej	least
malpli	less
malvarmumo	cold (illness)
mamo	breast
mamulo	mammal
mamzono	bra
mano	hand
manĝaĵo	food, something to eat
manĝi	to eat
manĝoĉambro	dining room
manki	to be lacking
manko	lack
mansaketo	handbag
mantelo	coat
mapo	map
maristo	sailor
maro	sea
marŝi	to walk
marŝmalo	marshmallow
martelo	hammer
matenmanĝo	breakfast

mateno	morning
meblo	(piece of) furniture
meleagro	turkey (bird)
melongeno	eggplant
melono	melon
mem (*mi mem*)	-self, -selves (myself)
memori	to remember
mentono	chin
menuo	menu
mesaĝo	message
meti	to put
metro	meter (metric)
metroo	subway
meza	middle
mezepoka	medieval
mi	I
mia	my
mielo	honey
mieno	(facial) expression
min	me
ministro	minister (political)
minuto	minute (time)
mirinda	amazing
misi	to be amiss
Kio misas?	What's wrong?
modo	fashion, style
molaro	molar (tooth)
monato	month
mondo	world
monero	coin (money)
mono	money

montaro	mountain chain
monto	mountain
montri	to show
mopedo	moped
morgaŭ	tomorrow
moruo	cod (fish)
moskeo	mosque
moskito	mosquito
motorciklo	motorcycle
motoro	motor
multa	many
multekosta	expensive
muro	wall
muso	mouse
mustardo	mustard
mustelo	weasel
muŝo	fly (insect)
muzeo	museum
muziko	music

N

naĝado	swimming
naĝi	to swim
najbaro	neighbor
naski	to give birth
naskiĝi	to be born
naskiĝtago	birthday
nazo	nose
naztuko	handkerchief
ne	no, not

nebulo	fog
necesa	necessary
necesejo	restroom
necesi	to be necessary
neĝero	snowflake
neĝi	to snow
neĝo	snow
nek	neither/nor
nenia	no kind of
nenial	for no reason
neniam	never
nenie	nowhere
neniel	in no way
nenies	no one's
nenio	nothing
neniom	no amount
neniu	no one
nepo	grandson
nepre	without fail
nevo	nephew
ni	we
nia	our
nigra	black
nin	us
nokto	night
noktomezo	midnight
nomi	to name something
nomiĝi	to be named
nomo	name
norda	northern
norden	northward

nordo	north
noto	note
nova	new (not old)
nubo	cloud
nuda	naked, bare
nul	zero
nun	now
nur	only
nutraĵo	food, nourishment
nutri	to nourish

O

oficejo	office
ofta	common
ofte	often
oleo	oil
okazo	occasion
okazi	to happen, occur
okcidenta	western
okcidenten	westward
okcidento	the west
okulo	eye
okupi	to occupy
okupita	occupied, busy
omaro	lobster
omleto	omelette
ondo	wave (sea, etc.)
oni	one, people, they
onklo	uncle

opinii	to have an opinion
opinio	opinion
ora	golden
oranĝa	orange (color)
oranĝo	orange (fruit)
ordo	order
en ordo	okay
orelo	ear
orienta	eastern
orienten	eastward
oriento	East, the Orient
oro	gold
ortangula	rectangular
osto	bone
ovo	egg

P

paco	peace
pagi	to pay
pago	apayment
paĝo	page
pala	pale (in color)
palaco	palace
palpebro	eyelid
palto	overcoat
pano	bread
panero	bread crumb
pantalono	pants
papilio	butterfly

parenco	relative, relation
parenteze	by the way, parenthetically
parentezo	parenthesis
parfumo	perfume
paro	pair
paroli	to speak
parto	part
pasi	to pass (by)
pasporto	passport
pastaĵo	pastry
pastoringo	donut
pasero	sparrow
paŝi	to take a step
paŝo	step
pastoro	pastor, minister (religion)
patro	father
peco	piece
pensi	to think
penso	thought
peranto (*per* + *anto*)	agent
perdi	to lose
perdiĝi	to get lost
persiko	peach
persono	person
peti	to seek, request
mi petas	please
peza	heavy, weighty
pezi	to weigh
pico	pizza

piedfingro	toe
piedo	foot
pikniko	picnic
pilko	ball (in sports)
pinglo	pin
pinto	point
pipro	pepper
piro	pear
pizo(j)	pea(s)
placo	plaza, public square
plaĉi	to please
plado	dish
planedo	planet
plafono	ceiling
planko	floor
plano	plan
plena	full
plezuro	pleasure
plej	most
pli	more
plumo	pen, feather
plura(j)	several
pluvero	raindrop
pluvi	to rain
pluvo	rain
pluvombrelo	umbrella
pojno	wrist
polekso	thumb
pomarbo	apple tree
pomo	apple
popolo	people, nation

populara	popular
porcelana	china (dishes)
porĉiama	eternal, forever
(*por* + *ĉiam* + *-a*)	
pordo	door
porkaĵo	pork
porko	pig
porti	to carry
posedi	to possess
post	after
posttagmeze	in the afternoon
posttagmezo	afternoon
poŝo	pocket
poŝto	mail
poŝtoficejo	post office
povi	to be able, can
povo	ability
prava	correct, right
prave	correctly
pravi	to be right
preferi	to prefer
preferinda	preferable
preĝejo	church, place for prayer
preĝi	to pray
premio	prize
preni	to take
prepari	to prepare
preskaŭ	almost
preta	ready
prezenti	to introduce (a person)
prezo	price

printempo	springtime
profesoro	professor
proksime	nearby
proksimume	approximately
promeni	to go for a walk
promesi	to promise
proponi	to propose
proverbo	proverb
pruno	plum
prunti	to borrow, lend
pruntedoni	to lend
pruntepreni	to borrow
pugno	fist
pupo	doll
pura	clean, pure
purigi	to clean
purpura	purple
puŝi	to push
puto	a well (n.)

R

rabeno	rabbi
radiofonio	radio (the medium)
radioricevilo	radio set, receiver
rajdi	to ride
rajti	to have the right
rampi	to crawl
rampulo	reptile
rano	frog
rapida	rapid, quick

rapide	quickly
rato	rat
razi	to shave
razilo	razor
regi	to rule
regiono	region
registaro	government
reĝo	king
rekomendi	to recommend
remizo	garage (at home)
rendevuo	meeting
reptilio	reptile
respondi	to answer
resti	to remain
restoracio	restaurant
retikulo	handbag
reto	net
reveni	to come back
revuo	magazine
riĉa	rich
rigardi	to look at
rikolto	harvest
ringo	ring
ripo	rib
ripozi	to rest
rizero	grain of rice
rizo	rice
robo	dress
rokenrolo	rock-'n'-roll (music)
ronda	round
rondo	ring, circle

rosmaro	walrus
roza	pink
rozo	rose (flower)
ruĝa	red
ruĝeta	reddish
rubo	rubbish, trash
rubujo	trash can
ruli	to roll

S

sacerdoto	priest
saĝa	wise
sako	bag
salato	salad
salikoko	shrimp
salmo	salmon
salo	salt
salono	living room
saluti	to greet
saluton	greetings, hi!
sama	same
sana	healthy
sandviĉo	sandwich
sango	blood
sano	health
sardelo	sardine
sata	full, satiated
saŭco	sauce
scii	to know something
scio	knowledge

scipovi	to know how to
sciuro	squirrel
sed	but
seĝo	chair
sekundo	second (time)
semajnfino	weekend
semajno	week
sen	without
sendi	to send
serĉi	to search, look for
serpento	snake
seruristo	locksmith
seruro	lock
servi	to serve
sezono	season (time)
si	him/her/itself; themselves
sia	his/her/its/their own
sidi	to sit
signifi	to mean
silento	silence
silko	silk
simio	monkey
sinjorino	Mrs., lady, ma'am
sinjoro	Mr., sir
sitelo	bucket
skatolo	box
skeleto	skeleton
sketi	to skate
skii	to ski
skio	ski

skribi	to write
skribilo	instrument for writing
skribotablo	desk
skvamo	scale (of fish, etc.)
sledoĉaro	sleigh
sofo	sofa
sola	alone
somero	summer
sonbendo	audio tape
sono	sound
speciala	special
spinaco	spinach
sporto	sport
stacidomo	railway station
stelo	star
stiri	to drive (a vehicle)
stomako	stomach
streko	dash, line
studento	student
studi	to study
stufaĵo	stew
stulta	stupid
stulteco	stupidity
stultulo	moron, stupid person
sub	under
subite	suddenly
submarŝipo	submarine
subtaso	saucer
subvesto	underwear
suda	southern
suden	southward

sudo	the South
sufiĉe	sufficiently, enough
sufikso	suffix
sugesti	to suggest
sukero	sugar
suko	juice
sunleviĝo	sunrise
suno	sun
supo	soup
sur	on
surbendigi	to record on tape
surfi	to surf
svingi	to swing

Ŝ

ŝafo	sheep
ŝajni	to seem
ŝajno	appearance, seeming
ŝako	chess
ŝalti	to switch on
(malŝalti)	(to switch off)
ŝaltilo	a switch
ŝampinjono	mushroom
ŝampuo	shampoo
ŝanĝi	to change
ŝarko	shark
ŝati	to prize, like, regard highly
ŝerci	to joke

ŝi	she
ŝia	her (possessive)
ŝin	her (direct object)
ŝinko	ham
ŝipo	ship
ŝlosi	to lock
ŝlosilo	key
ŝnureto	string
ŝnuro	rope
ŝorto	shorts (clothing)
ŝoseo	highway
ŝovi	to push along, slide
ŝranko	cupboard
ŝraŭbilo	screwdriver
ŝraŭbo	screw
ŝtato	state (political)
ŝteli	to steal
ŝtormo	storm
ŝtrumpeto	sock
ŝtrumpo	stocking
ŝtuparo	stairway
ŝtupo	step (stair)
ŝuldi	to owe
ŝuldo	debt
ŝultro	shoulder
ŝuo	shoe
ŝuti	to pour out
ŝveli	to swell up

T

tablo	table
tabulo	board
tagmanĝo	lunch
tagmezo	noon
tagiĝo	dawn ("becoming day")
tago	day
tajdo	tide
taksio	taxi
tapiŝo	rug
taso	cup
taŭga	fitting, suitable
taŭro	bull
taverno	tavern
teamo	team
teatraĵo	play (theater)
teatro	theater
telefono	telephone
telegramo	telegram
telesendi	to televise
televidilo	television set
televizio	television (the medium)
tempo	time
teniso	tennis
teo	tea
tero	earth
terpomo	potato
terura	terrible
terure	terribly, very
testudo	turtle, tortoise

tia	that kind of
(tia ĉi / ĉi tia)	this kind of
tial	for that reason
(tial ĉi / ĉi tial)	for this reason
tiam	then, at that time
(tiam ĉi / ĉi tiam)	at this time
tie	there, at that place
(tie ĉi / ĉi tie)	here, at this place
tiel	in that way
(tiel ĉi / ĉi tiel)	in this way
ties	that one's
(ĉi ties)	this one's
timi	to fear
tio	that thing
(tio ĉi / ĉi tio)	this thing
tiom	that quantity, that much
(tiom ĉi / ĉi tiom)	this quantity, this much
tipa	typical
tiri	to pull
tiu	that, that one
(tiu ĉi / ĉi tiu)	this, this one
toasto	toast (bread)
tolo	linen cloth
tolŝuo	tennis shoe, sneaker
tomato	tomato
tombejo	cemetery
tondro	thunder
tordi	to twist
tordiĝi	to get twisted
torto	pie
tra	through

traduki	to translate
trajno	(railroad) train
tranĉi	to cut
tranĉilo	knife
tre	very
trinkaĵo	beverage
trinki	to drink
tro	too much
trovi	to find
troviĝi	to be found, be located
truo	hole
truto	trout
tuj	immediately
tuko	cloth
tunelo	tunnel
turdo	thrush (bird)
turismo	tourism
turisto	tourist
turo	tower
tuta	the whole
tute	entirely, wholly

U

ulo	fellow, guy
ungo	nail (finger, toe)
universala	universal
universo	universe
urbano	city-dweller
urbestro	mayor (of city)
urbo	city

urso	bear
Usonano	United States citizen
Usono	United States of America
utila	useful
uvo	grape
uzi	to use
uzino	factory, plant

Ŭ

Note: The letter **ŭ** does not usually occur at the beginning of words; it most often combines with **a** or **e** (rarely **o**) to create diphthongs: *aŭ, eŭ (oŭ)*.

ŭa!	wah! (baby's cry)
ŭato	watt (electricity)

V

valizo	suitcase
valora	valuable
vampiro	vampire
vango	cheek
varbi	to recruit
varma	hot
varo	commodity
vasta	spacious, vast
vegetarano	vegetarian
veki	to wake someone
vekiĝi	to awake, wake up
vendejo	store

vendi	to sell
veni	to come
vento	wind
ventro	belly
vera	true
verda	green
vere	truly
verki	to compose, write
verkisto	writer
vero	truth
verŝi	to pour
vespermanĝo	dinner, evening meal
vespero	evening
vesperto	bat (animal)
vesto	article of clothing
veŝto	vest
vetero	weather
veturi	to go by vehicle
veturilo	vehicle
vi	you
via	your
viando	meat
vidaĵo	sight
vidbendo	videotape
videbla	visible
vidi	to see
vidvo	widower
vilaĝano	villager
vilaĝo	village, town
vin	you (direct object)
vinagro	vinegar

vino	wine
vintro	winter
viro	man
vitro	glass (substance)
vivi	to live
vizaĝo	face
viziti	to visit
vizo	visa
vojaĝi	to travel
vojo	road
voki	to call
voli	to want
vortaro	dictionary
vorto	word
vosto	tail
vulpo	fox

Z

zebro	zebra
zipo	zipper
zodiako	zodiac
zono	belt
zorgi	to care for, be concerned about
zumi	to hum, buzz

ENGLISH-ESPERANTO DICTIONARY
Angla-Esperanto Vortaro

Because English words such as "close" and "open" have no formal connection between them, we have listed them separately. The Esperanto translations, *fermi* and *malfermi* are obviously from the same root.

A

abdomen	abdomeno
to be able	povi
academy	akademio
(bank) account	konto
act	akto
active	aktiva
actor	aktoro
address	adreso
afternoon	tagmezo
again	denove
age	aĝo
agent	peranto
to agree	konsenti
to aim for	celi
air	aero
aircraft	aviadilo
already	jam
airplane	avio
airport	flughaveno, aeroporto
all (the whole)	tuta

alligator	aligatoro
almost	preskaŭ
alone	sola
always	ĉiam
amazing	mirinda
ambulance	ambulanco
America	Ameriko
(to be) amiss	misi
amphibian	amfibio
anchovy	anĉovo
and	kaj
animal	besto
ankle	maleolo
annoyance	ĝeno
to answer	respondi
ant	formiko
to applaud	aplaŭdi
apple	pomo
apple tree	pomarbo
appointment	rendevuo
approximately	proksimume
apricot	abrikoto
arch	arko
aria	ario
arm	brako
armchair	brakseĝo
to arrive	alveni
to ask	demandi
asparagus	asparago
association	asocio
at	ĉe

at all	ajn
anything at all	io ajn
to attend	ĉeesti
attention	attento
attentively	attenteme
aunt	onklino
auto(mobile)	aŭto
autumn	aŭtuno
to have available	disponi
away	for
to go away	foriri

B

baby	bebo
back (anatomy)	dorso
bad	malbona
bag	sako
bagel	kringo
to bake	baki
baker	bakisto
bakery	bakejo
ball (sports)	pilko
bank	banko
bare (naked)	nuda
baseball (the sport)	basbalo
baseball (the ball)	basbala pilko
basket	korbo
basketball (the sport)	basketbalo
basketball (the ball)	basketbala pilko
bat (animal)	vesperto

bat (sports)	klabo
bath	bano
bathroom	banĉambro
to be	esti
beak	beko
bean (flat, broad)	febo
bean (string, green)	fazeolo
beard	barbo
bearded man	barbulo
beautiful	bela
beauty	belo, beleco
beauty shop	kosmetikejo
because	ĉar
bed	lito
(to go to) bed	enlitiĝi
(to get out of) bed	ellitiĝi
beer	biero
before	antaŭ
to begin	komenci
being (creature)	estaĵo
to believe	kredi
belly	ventro
belt	zono
bench	benko
bicycle	biciklo
big	granda
bird	birdo
bishop	episkopo
black	nigra
blond	blonda
blood	sango

blood vessel	angio
blouse	bluzo
blue	blua
blue jeans	ĝinzo
board	tabulo
boat	boato
body	korpo
bone	osto
book	libro
boot	boto
to borrow	prunti, pruntepreni
both	ambaŭ
both...and...	kaj...kaj...
bottle	botelo
boy	knabo
bowl	bovlo
box	skatolo
bra	mamzono
brain	cerbo
bread	pano
bread crumb	panero
breakfast	matenmanĝo
breast	mamo
to bring	alporti
broccoli	brokolo
brother	frato
brown	bruna
brush	broso
bucket	sitelo
bull	taŭro, virbovo
burger	burgo

bus	aŭtobuso
business	afero, komerco
businessman	komercisto
but	sed
to butcher	buĉi
butter	butero
butterfly	papilio
buttock	gluteo
to buy	aĉeti
to buzz	zumi

C

cabbage	brasiko
cake	kuko
to calculate	kalkuli
to call	voki
Canada	Kanado
Canadian	kanada
Canadian man	Kanadano
candle	kandelo
cap	ĉapo, kaskedo
capital city	ĉefurbo
card	karto
to care for, nurse	zorgi
carrot	karoto
carousel	karuselo
to carry	porti
cart	ĉaro
cat	kato
cathedral	katedralo

cauliflower	florbrasiko
ceiling	plafono
to celebrate	celebri
celery	celerio
cell	ĉelo
cell phone	ĉela telefono
cement	cemento
cemetery	tombejo
to censure	cenzuri
cent (U.S. coin)	cendo
center	centro
central	centra
century	jarcento
(hot) cereal	kaĉo
certain, sure	certa
certainly	certe
chair	seĝo
chaos	ĥaoso
check (bank)	ĉeko
check (in restaurant, etc.)	kalkulo
cheek	vango
cherry	ĉerizo
chest (anatomy)	brusto
chest (box)	kesto
chicken (animal)	koko
chicken (meat)	kokaĵo
chief	ĉefa
child	infano
chin	mentono
china (dishes)	porcelana

China	Ĉinio
Chinese (pertaining to China)	ĉinia
Chinese man	Ĉino
chocolate	ĉokolado
choir	ĥoro
to choose	elekti
chorale	ĥoralo
church	preĝejo
cider	cidro
cigar	cigaro
cigarette	cigaredo
cinnamon	cinamo
circle	rondo
circus	cirko
to cite	citi
city	urbo
civilization	civilizacio
clean	pura
clock	horloĝo
to close	fermi
cloth	tuko
clothing	vesto
cloud	nubo
coat	mantelo, palto
cod (fish)	moruo
code	kodo
coffee	kafo
coffee house	kafejo
coin	monero

cold (temperature)	malvarma, frida
cold (illness)	malvarmumo
colleague	kolego
color	koloro
to come	veni
to come back	reveni
to come from	deveni
to comment	komenti
compact disk (CD)	kompakta disko (KD)
completely	tute
computer	komputoro, komputilo
to condemn	mallaŭdi
congratulations!	gratulon!
congress	kongreso
constellation	konstelacio
contents	enhavo
to cook	kuiri
to correspond	korespondi
to cost	kosti
cotton	kotono
couch	kanapo
country	lando
countryside	kamparo
courage	kuraĝo
courtyard	korto
cousin	kuzo (m.), kuzino (f.)
cow	bovino
crab	krabo
to crawl	rampi
cream	kremo

to create	krei
credit	kredito
crocodile	krokodilo
crow (bird)	korvo
cucumber	kukumo
to cultivate	kultivi
to cure	kuraci
customs (at border)	dogano
customs officer	doganisto
to cut	tranĉi
cycle	ciklo

D

danger	danĝero
dark (not bright)	malluma
dark (color)	malhela
date	dato
daughter	filino
dawn	tagiĝo
day	tago
debit	debeto
debt	ŝuldo
decade	jardeko
deed (action)	faro
deer	cervo
degree (temperature)	grado
delegate	delegito
dentist	dentisto
dentistry	dentomedicino
desert	dezerto

to desire	deziri
dessert	deserto
devil	diablo
diaper	bebtuko
dictionary	vortaro
different	malsama
difficult	malfacila
dinner	vespermanĝo
direct	direkta
director	direktoro
dirty	malpura
disc (disk)	disko
dish	plado
distance	distanco
to disturb	ĝeni
diverse	diversa
to do	fari
dog	hundo
doll	pupo
dollar	dolaro
donut	pastoringo
door	pordo
doubt	dubo
to doubt	dubi
to download	elŝuti
dress	robo
to dress	vestiĝi
to drive	stiri
drop (of water, etc.)	guto
drunk (inebriated)	ebria
duck	anaso

duckling	anasido
to dwell	loĝi
(live someplace)	

E

eagle	aglo
ear	orelo
early	frua
earth	tero
east (the East)	oriento
eastern	orienta
eastward	orienten
easy	facila
to eat	manĝi
eel	angilo
egg	ovo
eggplant	melongeno
either...or...	aŭ...aŭ...
elbow	kubuto
electricity	elektro
elegant	eleganta
elephant	elefanto
elevator	lifto
elsewhere	aliloka
empty	malplena
to end	finiĝi, malkomenci
engineer	inĝeniero
England	Anglio
English	angla
in English	angle, en la angla

Englishman	Anglo
to enjoy	ĝui
enough	sufiĉe
to enter	eniri
enthusiasm	entuziasmo
entrance	enirejo
epoch	epoko
to hold in esteem	estimi
Europe	Eŭropo
evening	vespero
ever	iam
everlasting	porĉiama
every amount	ĉiom
everybody's	ĉies
every kind	ĉia
everyone	ĉiu
(for) every reason	ĉial
everything	ĉio
every time	ĉiam
(in) every way	ĉiel
everywhere	ĉie
exact	ĝusta
to exist	ekzisti
exit	elirejo
to exit	eliri
expensive	multekosta, kostema
expression (on face)	mieno
eye	okulo
eyebrow	brovo
eyelid	palpebro

F

fable	fable
face	vizaĝo
fact	fakto
in fact	fakte
factory	fabriko, uzino
fairy tale	fabelo
familiar	konata
familiarity	kono
family	familio
famous	fama
to fare	farti
farm	bieno
farmer	bienisto, terkultivisto
fashion, style	modo
fashionable	laŭmoda
festival	festo
fever	febro
field	kampo
figure (number)	cifero
file	dosiero
film	filmo
to finish (something)	fini
fire	fajro
fish	fiŝo
to fish	fiŝi, fiŝkapti
fisherman	fiŝisto, fiŝkaptisto
fishing	fiŝkaptado
fist	pugno
fitting	deca

flag	flago
flake	floko
flap	klapo
floor (of a room)	planko
floor (of a building)	etaĝo
flounder (fish)	fleso
flower	floro
flu	gripo
fly (insect)	muŝo
to fly	flugi
fog	nebulo
food	nutraĵo, manĝaĵo
foot	piedo
forest	arbaro
foreword	antaŭparolo
to forget	forgesi
fork	forko
forward	antaŭen
fox	vulpo
France	Francio
free (not restricted)	libera
free (not occupied)	malokupita, libera
free time	libertempo
free (without cost)	senkosta, senpaga
to freeze	frosti
French	franca
in French	france, en la franca
Frenchman	Franco
friend	amiko
frog	rano
from	de, el

fruit	frukto
full	plena
full (having eaten enough)	sata
to function	funkcii
fundamental	fundamenta
furnishings	meblaro
furniture (a piece of)	meblo

G

galaxy	galaksio
galery	galerio
galoshes	galoŝoj
garage (at home)	remizo
garage (for repairs)	garaĝo
garbanzo (bean)	kikero
garden	ĝardeno
garlic	ajlo
gas	gaso
gauge	gaŭĝo
gene	geno
general (military rank)	generalo
general (not specific)	ĝeneralo
generous	malavara
ghost	fantomo
gift	donaco
girl	knabino
to give	doni
to give as a gift	donaci
to give away	fordoni

glass (for drinking)	glaso
glass (substance)	vitro
glove	ganto
glue	gluo
to go	iri
to go (by vehicle)	veturi
to go away	foriri
to go down	malsupreniri
to go in	eniri
to go out	eliri
to go up	supreniri
to go with	kuniri
goal	celo, golo (sports)
goat	kapro
god	dio
goddess	diino
gold	oro
golden	ora
good	bona
good-hearted	bonkora
goose	ansero
government	registaro
grammar	gramatiko
grandchildren	genepoj
granddaughter	nepino
grandfather	avo
grandmother	avino
grandson	nepo
grape	uvo, vinbero
grapefruit	grapfrukto
grasshopper	akrido

gray	griza
green	verda
to greet	saluti
greeting	saluto
to groan	ĝemi
guarantee	garantio
guest	gasto
to guide	gvidi
guy	ulo

H

hair (a strand of)	haro
hair	hararo
halibut	hipogloso
halo	aŭreolo
ham	ŝinko
hand	mano
handbag	mansaketo, retikulo
handkerchief	poŝtuko, naztuko
to happen	okazi
happily	feliĉe
happy	feliĉa
hare	leporo
harvest	rikolto
hat	ĉapelo
to have	havi
hawk	akcipitro
he	li
head	kapo
health	sano

healthy	sana, bonsana
to hear	aŭdi
heart	koro
heartfelt	elkora
heavy	peza
heel	kalkulo
hello	saluton
to help	helpi
hen	kokino
her (direct object)	ŝin
her/hers (possessive)	ŝia
here	ĉi tie / tie ĉi
here's...	jen...
high	alta
high school	liceo
him	lin
to hinder	malhelpi
his	lia
history	historio
hole	truo
holiday	ferio
home	hejmo
at home	hejme
homeward	hejmen
honey	mielo
hoof	hufo
to hope	esperi
horse	ĉevalo
horseshoe	huffero
hospital	hospitalo
hot	varma

hot dog	frankfurto
hotel	hotelo
hour	horo
house	domo
how	kiel
how much/many	kiom
to hum	zumi
human	homa
human being	homo
humanity	homaro
hundred	cent
hunger	malsato
hungry	malsata
to be hungry	malsati
to hunt	ĉasi
hunter	ĉasisto
hunting	ĉasado
to hurt	dolori
husband	edzo

I

I	mi
ice	glacio
to (turn into) ice	glaciiĝi
iceberg	glacimonto
ice cream	glaciaĵo
ice cube	glacikubo
iced tea	glaciteo
icy	glacia, frosta, malvarmega

idea	ideo
ill	malsana
to be ill	malsani
illness	malsano
imam	imamo
immediately	tuj
to include	inkluzivi
indeed	ja
inebriated	ebria
inexpensive	malmultekosta
to injure (something)	dolorigi
iron (metal)	fero
insect	insekto
to install	instali
instrument	ilo
intelligent	inteligenta
to intend	intenci
interesting	interesa
to introduce (a person)	prezenti
to introduce (a topic, etc.)	enkonduki
it	ĝi
it (direct object)	ĝin
its	ĝia

J

jacket	jako
Japan	Japanio
Japanese	japana
in Japanese	japane, en la japana

Japanese man	Japano
jargon	ĵargono
jazz	ĵazo
jealous	ĵaluza
jeans (pants)	ĝinzo
jeep	ĵipo
jelly	ĵeleo
joint (anatomy)	artikolo
joke	ŝerco
to joke	ŝerci
joy	ĝojo
joyful	ĝoja
to juggle	ĵongli
juice	suko
jungle	ĝangalo
just (fair)	justa
just a moment ago	ĵus

K

kerchief	kaptuko
ketchup	keĉupo
kidney	reno
kilogram	kilogramo
kilometer	kilometro
kind (goodhearted)	afabla
kind (sort)	speco
(be so) kind (as to)	bonvolu
king	reĝo
kiss	kiso
to kiss	kisi

kitchen	kuirejo
to knead	knedi
knee	genuo
knife	tranĉilo
to know (someone)	koni
to know (a fact)	scii
knowledge	scio

L

lack	manko
to be lacking	manki
lady	sinjorino
ladybird beetle	kokcinelo
lake	lago
lamp	lampo
language	lingvo
late (not early)	malfrua
lavatory	lavejo
lawn	gazono
to lay (eggs)	demeti
leader	estro
to learn	lerni
least	(la) malplej
left (left hand, left side)	maldekstra
leg	kruro
lemon	citrono
lemonade	limonado
to lend	prunti, pruntedoni
less	malpli
letter (of alphabet)	litero

letter (to mail)	letero
lettuce	laktuko
library	biblioteko
to lift	levi
light (in weight)	malpeza
light (in color)	hela
light (bright)	luma, lumplena
lightening	fulmo
linen	tolo
lion	leono
lip	lipo
list	listo
to listen	aŭskulti
little	malgranda, eta
a little bit	iomete
to live (exist)	vivi
to live (somewhere)	loĝi
liver	hepato
living room	salono, vivoĉambro, loĝoĉambro
lizard	lacerto
lobster	omaro
lock	seruro
locksmith	seruristo
locust (insect)	lokusto
long	longa
to look at	rigardi
to lose	perdi
to get lost	perdiĝi
low (not high)	malalta

lunch	tagmanĝo, lunĉo
to do lunch	tagmanĝi, lunĉi

M

magazine	gazeto, revuo
mail	poŝto
to make, do	fari
mammal	mamulo
man	viro
mankind	la homaro
many	multa
map	mapo
market	bazaro, vendoplaco
to marry	geedziĝi
to marry a man	edzigi
to marry a woman	edzinigi
marshmallow	marŝmalo
match (for fire)	alumeto
to matter	gravi
mayonnaise	majonezo
mayor (of a city)	urbestro
me	min
mean (disagreeable)	malafabla
to mean	signifi
meeting	kunsido, rendevuo
melon	melono
member (of group)	ano, membro
menu	menuo, manĝokarto
mermaid	marvirino

message	mesaĝo
middle	meza
Middle Ages	Mezepoko
midnight	noktomezo
milk	lakto
millennium	jarmilo
Miss	Fraŭlino
molar	molaro
money	mono
monkey	simio
month	monato
moon	luno
moonbeam	lun-aŭreolo
moped	mopedo
more	pli
morning	mateno
mosque	moskeo
mosquito	moskito
most	(la) plej
motor	motoro
motorcycle	motorciklo
mountain	monto
mountains	(in a chain) montaro
mouth	buŝo
movie house	kinejo
Mr.	Sinjoro
Mr. and Mrs.	Gesinjoroj
Mrs.	Sinjorino
museum	muzeo
mush	kaĉo
mushroom	ŝampinjono

music	muziko
musician	muzikisto
mustache	lipharoj
mustard	mustardo
my	mia

N

nail (hardware)	najlo
nail (finger/toe)	ungo
name	nomo
to name something	nomi
to be named	nomiĝi
napkin	buŝtuko
narrow	mallarĝa
necessary	necesa
to be necessary	necesi
neck	kolo
to need	bezoni
neighbor	najbaro
neither...nor...	nek...nek...
nephew	nevo
net	reto
never	neniam
new	nova
news	novaĵo
newspaper	ĵurnalo
niece	nevino
night	nokto
no	ne
no amount	neniom

no kind of	nenia
no one	neniu
no one's	nenies
(for) no reason	nenial
(in) no way	neniel
noon	tagmezo
north	nordo
northern	norda
northward	norden
nose	nazo
not	ne
note	noto
notebook	notlibro, kajero
nothing	nenio
to nourish	nutri
nourishment	nutraĵo
now	nun
nowhere	nenie
to nurse (to health)	flegi
nurse	flegist(in)o

O

obligation	devo
to be obliged to	devi
occasion	okazo, fojo (a time)
occupied	okupita
to occupy	okupi
to occur	okazi
of	de
office	oficejo, kantoro

offspring	ido(j)
often	ofte
oil	oleo
old (not new)	malnova
old (not young)	maljuna
omelette	omleto
once, at one time	unfoje
one (people, they)	oni
onion	cepo
only	nur
to open	malfermi
opinion	opinio
to have an opinion	opinii
or	aŭ
orange (color)	oranĝa, oranĝkolorra
orange (fruit)	oranĝo
to order	ordi
order	ordo
everything in order	ĉio en ordo
other	alia
on the other hand	aliflanke
our	nia
overcoat	palto
to owe	ŝuldi

P

package	pako
pain	doloro
pair	paro
palace	palaco

pale	pala
pants	pantalono
parenthesis	parentezo
parenthetically	parenteze
parents	gepatroj
part	parto
to pass	pasi
passport	pasporto
pastor	pastoro
to pay	pagi
payment	pago
peace	paco
peach	persiko
pear	piro
peas	pizoj
pen	plumo, skribilo
people (nation)	popolo
pepper	pipro
pepperoni	kajenkolbaso
perfume	parfumo
perhaps	eble
person	persono
pharmacist	apotekisto
pharmacy	apoteko
physician	kuracisto
picnic	pikniko
picture	bildo
pie	torto
piece	peco
pig	porko
pin	pinglo

pineapple	ananaso
pink	roza, rozkolora
pizza	pico
place	loko
planet	planedo
to play	ludi
play (theater)	teatraĵo
plaza	placo
please	mi petas
to please	plaĉi
pleasure	plezuro
plum	pruno
pocket	poŝo
point	pinto
polite	ĝentila
poor	malriĉa
poorly	malbone
popular	populara
pork	porkaĵo
to possess	posedi
post office	poŝtoficejo
potato	terpomo
sweet potato	batato
to pour	verŝi
to praise	laŭdi
to pray	preĝi
to prefer	preferi
preferable	preferebla
to prepare	prepari
to be present	ĉeesti
price	prezo

pride	fiero
priest	sacerdoto
prince	princo
princess	princino
prize	premio
professor	profesoro
to promise	promesi
proud	fiera
proverb	proverbo
to pull	tiri
purple	purpura
to push	puŝi
to put	meti

Q

queen	reĝino
question	demando
quick	rapida
quick!	ek!
quickly	rapide
quotation	cito
to quote	citi
open quote	cit
close quote	malcit

R

rabbi	rabeno
rabbit	kuniklo
radio (the medium)	radiofonio

radio set, receiver	radioricevilo
rain	pluvo
to rain	pluvi
rainbow	ĉielarko
raincoat	pluvmantelo
rarely	malofte
rat	rato
razor	razilo
to read	legi
ready	preta
(for that) reason	tial
to recommend	rekomendi
to recount	rakonti
rectangular	ortangula
red	ruĝa
reddish	ruĝeta
reel (spool, bobbin)	bobeno
refrigerator	fridujo
to regard highly	ŝati
region	regiono
to remain	resti
to remember	memori
to repeat	ripeti
reptile	rampulo, reptilio
to request	peti
to respond	respondi
to rest	ripozi
the rest, remaining	cetera
restaurant	restoracio
restroom	necesejo
to retire	eksiĝi

to return (something bought)	malaĉeti
rib	ripo
rice	rizo
rich	riĉa
to ride	rajdi
right (not left)	dekstra
right (not wrong)	prava
right (e.g. civil rights)	rajto
to be right	pravi
to have the right	rajti
ring	ringo
to rise	leviĝi
roach	blato
rock-'n'-roll	rokenrolo
to roll	ruli
room	ĉambro
rooster	koko, virkoko
rope	ŝnuro
rose (flower)	rozo
round	ronda
rude	malĝentila
rug	tapiŝo
to rule	regi

S

sad	malĝoja, malgaja
salad	salato
salt	salo
same	sama

sandwich	sandviĉo
sardine	sardelo
satiated	sata
sauce	saŭco
sausage	kolbaso
to say	diri
scale (on fish, etc.)	skvamo
school	lernejo
screw	ŝraŭbo
screwdriver	ŝraŭbilo
sea	maro
seal (animal)	foko
to search for	serĉi
season (of the year)	sezono
to seat (someone)	sidigi
to be seated	sidiĝi
second (of time)	sekundo
to see	vidi
to see again	revidi, vidi denove
-self (myself)	mem (*mi mem*)
to sell	vendi
to seem	ŝajni
to sense	senti
serious	grava
to serve	servi
several	plura(j)
shackles	kateno
shark	ŝarko
to shave	razi (sin)
she	ŝi
sheep	ŝafo

to shine	brili
ship	ŝipo
shirt	ĉemizo
shoe	ŝuo
short (not long)	mallonga
shorts (clothing)	ŝorto
shoulder	ŝultro
to show	montri
shrimp	salikoko
sign	signo
silence	silento
silk	silko
silken	silka
silver (color)	arĝenta
silver (metal)	arĝento
since	ekde
to sing	kanti
sister	fratino
to sit	sidi
skate (ice)	sketŝuo
skate (on wheels)	rulsketŝuo
to skate (on ice)	sketi
to skate (on wheels)	rulsketi
skeleton	skeleto
ski	skio
to ski	skii
skin	haŭto
skirt	jupo
sky	ĉielo
slow	malrapida
to smoke	fumi

snail	helikoko
snake	serpento
sneaker, tennis shoe	tolŝuo
snow	neĝo
to snow	neĝi
soccer	futbalo
soccer ball	futbala pilko
sock	ŝtrumpeto
sofa	sofo
some amount	iom
some kind of	ia
someone	iu
someone's	ies
(for) some reason	ial
something	io
sometime	iam
(in) some way	iel
somewhere	ie
son	filo
soon	baldaŭ
sound	sono
south (the South)	sudo
southern	suda
southward	suden
Spain	Hispanio
Spaniard	Hispano
Spanish	hispana
in Spanish	hispane, en la hispana
sparrow	pasero
to speak	paroli
special	speciala

spice	spico
spider	araneo
spiderweb	araneaĵo
spinach	spinaco
spoon	kulero
sport	sporto
to spread	disvastigi
spring (season)	printempo
square	kvadrata
squirrel	sciuro
stairway	ŝtuparo
star	stelo
state (condition)	stato
state (political)	ŝtato
(train) station	stacidomo
steak	bifsteko
to steal	ŝteli
step	paŝo
to (take a) step	paŝi
step (stair)	ŝtupo
stew	stufaĵo
still, yet	ankoraŭ
stingy	avara
stocking	ŝtrumpo
stomach	stomako
store	vendejo, butiko
storm	ŝtormo
strawberry	frago
string	ŝnureto
student	lernanto

student (university)	studento
to study	studi
stupid	stulta, malinteligenta
stupid person	stultulo, malinteligentulo
stupidity	stulteco, malinteligenteco
submarine	submarŝipo
to subscribe	aboni
subscriber	abonanto
subscription	abono
subway	metroo
suddenly	subite
suffix	sufikso
sugar	sukero
suitable	taŭga
to be suitable	taŭgi
suitcase	valizo
to suggest	sugesti
sun	suno
sunrise	sunleviĝo
sunset	sunsubiĝo
superfluous	malnecesa
to surf	surfi
surfboard	surfotabulo
swallow (bird)	hirundo
swan	cigno
to swear (an oath)	ĵuri
to swell	ŝveli
to swim	naĝi
to swing	svingi

T

tail (of animal)	vosto
to take	preni
tape	(in general) bendo
tape (adhesive)	glubendo
tape (recording)	sonbendo
tape recorder	magnetofono
to taste (something)	gustumi
to (have the) taste	gusti
tavern	taverno
taxi	taksio
tea	teo
teabag	tesaketo
teapot	tekruĉo
to teach	instrui
teacher (in general)	instruanto
teacher (professional)	instruisto
team	teamo
to televise	telesendi
television set	televidilo
television (the medium)	televizio
terrible	terura
textbook	lernolibro
to thank	danki
thanks	dankon
that	tiu
that amount	tuom
that kind	tia
that one	tiu
that one's	ties

(for) that reason	tial
(in) that way	tiel
the	la
their	ilia
them	ilin
then	tiam
there	tie
they	ili
thief	ŝtelisto
to think	pensi
this	ĉi tiu / tiu ĉi
this amount	ĉi tiom
this kind	ĉi tia
this one	ĉi tiu
this one's	ĉi ties
(for) this reason	ĉi tial
(in) this way	ĉi tiel
to throw	ĵeti
thrush (bird)	turdo
thumb	polekso
thunder	tondro
thus, therefore	do
tick (insect)	iksodo
ticket	bileto
ticket window	giĉeto
tide	tajdo
time (duration, general)	tempo
time (an instance, occasion)	fojo
at times	foje
toad	bufo

toast (bread)	toasto, rostita pano
today	hodiaŭ
token	ĵetono
tomato	tomato
tomorrow	morgaŭ
tongue (anatomy)	lango
too much	tro
tooth	dento
tourism	turismo
tourist	turisto
toy	ludilo
to translate	traduko
translation	traduko, tradukado
translator	tradukisto
trash	rubo
trash can	rubujo
to travel	vojaĝi
tree	arbo
trout	truto
truck	kamiono
true	vera
truth	vero
tub (bathtub)	kuvo, bankuvo, banujo
tunnel	tunelo
turkey (bird)	meleagro
turtle	testudo
twin	ĝemelo
to twist	tordi
to get twisted	tordiĝi
type	tipo
typical	tipa

U

ugly	malbela
umbrella	(pluv)ombrelo
uncle	onklo
under	sub
underpants	kalsoneto
to understand	kompreni
understandably	kompreneble
underwear	subvesto
unfortunately	malfeliĉe
unimportant	malgrava
United States	Usono
United States citizen	Usonano
universal	universala
universe	universo
unmarried man	fraŭlo
until	ĝis
us	nin
to use	uzi
useful	utila
to be useful	utili
usually	kutime

V

valuable	valora
to value	valori
vampire	vampiro
vast	vasta
vegetable	legomo

vegetarian	vegetarano
(blood) vessel	angio
vest	veŝto
videotape	vidbendo
videotape recorder (VCR)	aŭdvida magnetofono
village	vilaĝo
villager	vilaĝano
visa	vizo
visible	videbla
to visit	viziti

W

wah! (baby's cry)	ŭah!
to wait	atendi
waiter	kelnero
waitress	kelnerino
to wake (someone)	veki
to wake up	vekiĝi
to walk	marŝi, piediri
to go for a walk	promeni
wall	muro
walrus	rosmaro
to want	voli
wares (goods)	varoj
to warn	averti
warning	averto
to wash	lavi
to get washed	laviĝi
washbasin	lavujo, lavkuvo

watch out!	atenton!
water	akvo
watt (electricity)	ŭato, vato
wave (water)	ondo
we	ni
weasel	mustelo
weather	vetero
week	semajno
weekend	semajnfino
welcome!	bonvenon
to welcome	bonvenigi
well	bone
well (for water, etc.)	puto
werewolf	lupfantomo
west	okcidento
western	okcidenta
westward	okcidenten
whale	baleno
what	kio
what kind of	kia
(in) what way	kiel
when	kiam
where	kie
which (one)	kiu
while	dum
white	blanka
who	kiu
whole (the whole, all)	tuta
whose	kies
why	kial
wide	larĝa

widow	vidvino
widower	vidvo
wife	edzino
wind (weather)	ventro
window	fenestro
wine	vino
wing	flugilo
winter	vintro
wisdom	saĝo, saĝeco
wise	saĝa
wiseman	saĝulo
with	kun
without	sen
wolf	lupo
woman	virino
word	vorto
to work	labori
worker	laboristo
world	mondo
the whole world	la tuta mondo
world-wide	tutmonda
worthy	inda
worthy of thanks	dankinda
wrist	pojno
wristwatch	brakhorloĝo
to write (in general)	skribi
to write (books, music)	verki
writer	verkisto

X

xenophobia	ksenofobio
xerography	kserografio
xylophone	ksilofono

Y

yam	ignamo
year	jaro
yellow	flava
yes	jes
yesterday	hieraŭ
to yield	cedi
yo-yo	ludbobeno
you	vi
you (direct object)	vin
young	juna
your	via

Z

zeal	fervoro
zebra	zebro
zero	nul
zip code	poŝta kodo
zipper	zipo
zither	citro
zodiac	zodiako
zoo	bestoĝardeno, zoologia ĝardeno

PART FOUR—THE PHRASEBOOK
Kvara Parto—La Esprimaro

GREETINGS AND USEFUL EXPRESSIONS
Salutoj kaj Utilaj Esprimoj

Good morning!	Bonan matenon!
Good day!	Bonan tagon!
Good evening!	Bonan vesperon!
Good night!	Bonan nokton!
Hi!	Saluton!
Welcome!	Bonvenon!
Welcome to Esperantoland!	Bonvenon al Esperantio!
Mr., sir	Sinjoro
Mrs., ma'am	Sinjorino
Miss	Fraŭlino
Fellow Esperantist	Samideano (*sam/a + ide/o + -an- + -o*)
How are you?	Kiel vi fartas?
How's everything?	Kiel ĉio?
What's new?	Kio nova?
(I am) fine, thanks.	(Mi fartas) bone, dankon.
Very well, thanks.	Tre bone, dankon.
Everything's fine!	Ĉio (estas) en ordo!
And you?	Kaj vi (Sinjoro/ Sinjorino/ Fraŭlino)?
Rather well, thanks.	Sufiĉe bone, dankon.
How's the family?	Kiel la familio fartas?
Everyone's fine, thanks.	Ĉiuj fartas bone, dankon.

MEETING PEOPLE
Konatiĝo

What is your name?	Kio estas via nomo?
My name is Peter.	Mia nomo estas Petro.
What is your name?	Kiel vi nomiĝas?
	(How are you named?)
My name is Machiko.	Mi nomiĝas Maĉiko.
	(I am named...)
Nice to meet you.	Estas plezuro konatiĝi
	kun vi.
Nice to meet you.	Estas plezuro.
(short version)	
The pleasure is mine.	La plezuro estas mia.
Let me introduce...	Mi prezentu al vi...
my husband.	mian edzon.
my wife.	mian edzinon.
my friend (male).	mian amikon.
my friend (female).	mian amikinon.
my associate.	mian kolegon.
Who is...	Kiu estas...
that man?	tiu viro?
that woman?	tiu virino?
that boy?	tiu knabo?
that girl?	tiu knabino?
That is...	Tiu estas...
my husband.	mia edzo.
my wife.	mia edzino.
a villager.	vilaĝano.
a girl from the town.	vilaĝanino.
Do you know Machiko?	Ĉu vi konas Maĉikon?
Yes, I (already) know	Jes, mi (jam) konas ŝin.
her.	
No, I don't know her.	Ne, mi ne konas ŝin.
Do you know her	Ĉu vi scias ŝian adreson?
address?	

Yes, I know it.	Jes, mi scias ĝin.
No, I don't know it.	Ne, mi ne scias ĝin.
Do you?	Ĉu vi?
I don't know.	Mi ne scias.
I think so.	Mi opinias, ke jes.
I don't think so.	Mi opinias, ke ne.
Do you know Richard?	Ĉu vi konas Rikardon?
No, I don't know him.	Ne, mi ne konas lin.
Is he an Esperantist?	Ĉu li estas Esperantisto?
Yes, I think he is.	Jes, mi kredas, ke li estas Esperantisto.
I guess you don't know his address, then.	Do, vi kompreneble ne scius lian adreson.
Whom do you know at this meeting?	Kiun vi konas ĉe tiu ĉi kunsido?
Almost no one.	Preskaŭ neniun.
Where are you from?	De kie vi estas?
I'm from the United States.	Mi estas de Usono.
Are you Canadian?	Ĉu vi estas Kanadano?
No, I'm a citizen of the United States.	Ne, mi estas Usonano.
Those ladies are citizens of the United States.	Tiuj sinjorinoj estas Usonaninoj.
The President of the United States will be traveling to China.	La usona Prezidento vojaĝos al Ĉinio.
I am a member of ELNA.	Mi estas ELNA-ano.
Are you an Esperantist?	Ĉu vi estas Esperantisto?

USEFUL LITTLE WORDS
Mallongaj vortoj tre utilaj

I agree.	Mi konsentas.
I disagree.	Mi ne konsentas.
I obstinately refuse.	Mi tute malkonsentas.
That's nonsense!	Tio estas volapukaĵo!

Note: Back in the early days of Esperanto, *Volapük* was a rival international language. Volapük has long since ceased to be used, but Esperantists keep alive the old sense of competition by referring to anything nonsensical as a *volapukaĵo*, "Volapük-thing."

Goodbye.	Ĝis revido.
Until next time.	Ĝis la revido.
	(until the re-seeing)
Bye!	Ĝis! (Ĝis la!)
Farewell!	Adiaŭ!
Bon voyage!	Bonan vojaĝon!
Congratulations!	Gratulon!
Yes.	Jes.
Yes, of course.	Jes, certe.
Yes, that's how it is.	Jes, tiel estas.
No, that's not how it is.	Ne, ne estas tiel.
No.	Ne.
Absolutely not!	Tute ne!
Maybe.	Eble.
It may be.	Povas esti.
Please.	Mi petas.
	(I request, seek)
Repeat that, please.	Ripetu tion, mi petas.
Thank you.	Dankon.
Thank you, ma'am.	Dankon, Sinjorino.
Thank you very much.	Multan dankon.

You're welcome.	Ne dankinde.
	(not worthy of thanks)
Excuse me (please).	Pardonu min (mi petas)!
I'm sorry.	Mi bedaŭras.
I beg your pardon.	Mi pardonpetas.
Do you speak...	Ĉu vi parolas...
Esperanto?	Esperanton?
English?	la anglan lingvon?
Japanese?	la japanan lingvon?
French?	la francan lingvon?
Spanish?	la hispanan lingvon?
Yes, a little.	Jes, iomete.
Yes, I speak	Jes, mi parolas
Esperanto...	Esperanton...
but I don't speak	sed mi ne parolas la
Japanese.	japanan.
Do you understand	Ĉu vi komprenas
Esperanto?	Esperanton?
I understand	Mi komprenas
Esperanto...	Esperanton...
but I don't understand	sed vin mi ne
you!	komprenas!
Did you understand?	Ĉu vi komprenis?
I think you misunder-	Mi pensas, ke vi
stand me.	miskomprenas min.
Are you proficient in	Ĉu vi scipovas la anglan?
English?	
Ha! There are two	Ho! Jen du
Esperantists speaking	Esperantistoj, kiuj
their native language	krokodilas!
with each other!	

Note: Of the expressions which have developed in Esperanto that are unique to the language, we find the verb *krokodili*, "to speak a national language when among Esperantists." Although the word *krokodilo* means "crocodile," this slang expression

USEFUL LITTLE WORDS

is among the most widely known and used in the language.

I have been studying Esperanto...	Mi studas Esperanton ekde...
for several weeks (months).	kelkaj semajnoj (monatoj).
Let me show you my poems.	Mi montru al vi miajn poemojn.
You are speaking too fast.	Vi parolas ja tro rapide.
Please speak more slowly.	Bonvolu paroli pli malrapide, mi petas.
You are listening too slowly.	Vi aŭskultas tro malrapide.
Please listen more carefully.	Bonvolu aŭskulti pli atenteme, mi petas.
Are you sure you're speaking as fast as possible?	Ĉu estas certe, ke vi parolas kiel eble plej rapide?
I can still catch a few words.	Iujn vortojn mi povas ankoraŭ kompreni.
I don't understand that word.	Tiun vorton mi ne komprenas.
Write it down, please.	Skribu ĝin, mi petas.
Please be so kind as to write it down	Bonvolu skribi ĝin, mi petas.
Alas, I forget!	Ho ve! Mi forgesas.
That doesn't matter.	Ne gravas.
Listen, I'll repeat.	Aŭskultu, mi ripetas.

The following expressions, used judiciously, will help you to seem more fluent in Esperanto than you may actually be. Sometimes, a small word, said at just the right moment, is worth more than an entire sentence.

USEFUL LITTLE WORDS

also, too	ankaŭ
me too	ankaŭ mi
How about you?	Ĉu vi ankaŭ?
me neither	nek mi
thus, so, therefore	do
Let's do it, then!	Ni faru tion do!
a little bit	iomete
a little bit farther on	iomete pli fora
well then, so	nu
So, as you were explaining	Nu, vi estis eksplikanta...
heading home, homeward	hejmen
in the countryside	en la kamparo
in the mountains	en la montaro
on the other side (hand)	aliflanke
by the way	parenteze
oh no!	ho ve!
only	nur
I have only thirty dollars.	Mi havas nur tridek dolarojn.
I'm the only one who has thirty dollars.	Nur mi havas tridek dolarojn.
perhaps	eble
it could be	povas esti...
One can't...	oni ne povas...
One doesn't have the right...	oni ne rajtas...
One can't swim here.	Oni ne povas naĝi ĉi tie.
One is not permitted to swim here.	Oni ne rajtas naĝi ĉi tie.
still	ankoraŭ
Are you still hungry?	Ĉu vi ankoraŭ malsatas?
then, at that time	tiam
Listen!	Aŭskultu!

Please listen!	Bonvolu aŭskulti!
Look!	Rigardu!
Don't look!	Ne rigardu!
Please don't look!	Bonvolu ne rigardi!
See here! / Look!	Vidu!
Wait!	Atendu!
Wait for me!	Atendu min!
Please don't bother to wait for me.	Bonvolu ne atendi min!
Pay attention! / Watch out!	Atentu!
Be quiet!	Silentu!
Please be quiet.	Bonvolu silenti!
there, in that place	tie
here, in this place	ĉi tie/tie ĉi (either way is fine)
at our place	ĉe ni
very	tre
very big	tre granda
very good	tre bona
very well	tre bone

Note: In Esperanto, as in all other languages, little words such as *tre* tend to loose their effectiveness through overuse. In everyday speech, one often hears other words, *terure* (terribly) for example, used to replace *tre*. We could also make an adverb from the suffix *-eg-* and say *ege*.

already	jam
I have (already) seen that play.	Mi jam vidis tiun teatraĵon.
too	tro
She talks too fast!	Ŝi parolas tro rapide!
enough	sufiĉe
Is it big enough?	Ĉu ĝi estas sufiĉe granda?

again, anew	denove
always	ĉiam
never	neniam
I never understand him.	Mi neniam komprenas lin.
never before	neniam antaŭe
(at) sometime	iam
Have you ever before attended a Universal Congress?	Ĉu vi iam antaŭe ĉeestis Universalan Kongreson?
No, never before.	Ne, neniam antaŭe.
in some way	iel ajn
often	ofte
rarely	malofte
soon	baldaŭ
suddenly	subite, ek-
They suddenly left.	Ili subite foriris. / Ili ekforiris.
early, late	frue, malfrue
something	io
Say something in Esperanto.	Diru ion Esperante.
everything	ĉio
nothing	nenio
He has an opinion about everything, but he understands nothing!	Li komentas ĉion, sed komprenas nenion!
somewhere	ie
immediately	tuj
Please respond immediately.	Bonvolu tuj respondi.
without fail	nepre
I'll remember your address.	Mi nepre memoros vian adreson.
without a doubt	sendube

so, in such a way/ manner	tiel
Chin up!	Kuraĝon!
Bravo!	Brave!
See you later!	Ĝis baldaŭ!
See you tomorrow!	Ĝis morgaŭ!
See you again!	Ĝis revido!

HOW DOES ONE SAY...?
Kiel oni diras...?

to say	diri
How does one say "book" in Esperanto?	Kiel oni diras "book" Esperante?
One says "libro."	Oni diras "libro."
How does one say "child"?	Kiel oni diras "child"?
For "child" one says "infano."	Por "child" oni diras "infano."
to mean, signify	signifi
What does "nova" mean?	Kion signifas "nova"?
"Nova" means "new."	"Nova" signifas "new."
Does "domo" mean mountain?	Ĉu "domo" signifas "mountain"?
No, not at all!	Ho tute ne!
"Domo" means "house."	"Domo" signifas "house."
I do not understand the meaning of this word.	Mi ne komprenas la signifon de ĉi tiu vorto.

INTERROGATIVE WORDS
Demandovortoj

The basic interrogative word for "yes/no" questions is *ĉu*. Word-order is not affected.

Do you speak Esperanto?	Ĉu vi parolas Esperanton?
You speak Esperanto, don't you?	Vi parolas Esperanton, ĉu ne?
She's an Esperantist, isn't she?	Ŝi estas Esperantisto, ĉu ne?

All other interrogative words in Esperanto begin with the letter **k**.

WHO?
Kiu? (plural: *Kiuj?*)

that person, that one	tiu (plural: tiuj)
this person, this one	tiu ĉi / ĉi tiu
no one	neniu
someone	iu
everyone	Ĉiu (plural: Ĉiuj)
Who is that?	Kiu estas tiu?
Who is that man?	Kiu estas tiu sinjoro?
Who is this man?	Kiu estas tiu ĉi sinjoro?
Who are those people?	Kiuj estas tiuj personoj?
To whom?	Al kiu?
To whom did you speak?	Al kiu vi parolis?
Whose?	De kiu? Kies?
that person's	ties
no one's	nenies
someone's	ies
everyone's	ĉies
Whose book is that?	Kies libro estas tiu? / De kiu estas tiu libro?
That's no one's book.	Tiu libro estas nenies.
Who has the book now?	Kiu nun havas la libron?
Whom did you see in the village?	Kiun vi vidis en la vilaĝo?

WHICH...?
Kiu...?

Which book is that one?	Kiu libro estas tiu?
That is my Esperanto textbook.	Tiu estas mia lernolibro pri Esperanto.
Which books are those?	Kiuj libroj estas tiuj?
Those are my dictionaries.	Tiuj estas miaj vortaroj.
Which sandwich did you buy?	Kiun sandviĉon vi aĉetis?
I bought the big one.	Mi aĉetis la grandan. / La grandan mi aĉetis.
Which flowers did you choose?	Kiujn florojn vi elektis?
I chose the red ones.	Mi elektis la ruĝajn. / La ruĝajn mi elektis.
What color is your house?	Kiukolora estas via domo?
My house is white.	Mia domo estas blanka.
What color are your rugs?	Kiukoloraj estas viaj tapiŝoj?
Our rugs are green.	Niaj tapiŝoj estas verdaj.
What sport do you prefer?	Kiun sporton vi preferas?
I prefer tennis.	Mi preferas tenison.

WHAT?
Kio?

that	tio
this	tio ĉi / ĉi tio
nothing	nenio
something	io
everything	ĉio
What is that?	Kio estas tio?
What is this thing?	Kio estas ĉi tiu aĵo?
What are you doing?	Kion vi faras?
I am studying Esperanto.	Mi studas Esperanton.
I am speaking Esperanto.	Mi parolas Esperante.
What is he doing?	Kion li faras?
What is she doing?	Kion ŝi faras?
She is playing soccer.	Ŝi ludas futbalon.
What are they doing?	Kion ili faras?
They are singing.	Ili kantas.
What shall we do?	Kion ni faru?
Let's read the newspaper!	Ni legu la ĵurnalon!
What does one usually prepare for breakfast?	Kion oni kutime preparas por la matenmanĝo?
One prepares coffee with milk, bread and butter.	Oni preparas kafon kun lakto kaj buterpanon.

WHERE?
Kie?

there	tie
here	tie ĉi / ĉi tie
nowhere	nenie
somewhere	ie
everywhere	ĉie
Where is the church?	Kie estas la preĝejo?
It is in the village.	Ĝi estas en la vilaĝo.
It is here.	Ĝi estas ĉi tie.
It is there.	Ĝi estas tie.
right	dekstra
left	maldekstra
It is on the right.	Ĝi estas je la dekstra.
It is on the left.	Ĝi estas ja la maldekstra.
Where am I?	Kie mi estas?
You are in Esperantoland!	Vi estas en Esperantio!
Where is he/she?	Kie li/ŝi estas?
Where are they?	Kie ili estas?
Where are you?	Kie vi estas?
Where to? To what place?	Kien? Al kiu loko?
Where are you going (to)?	Kien vi iras?
to the right	dekstren
to the left	maldekstren
I am going to my house.	Mi iras al mia domo.
Who is going home?	Kiu iras domon?
I (am).	Mi.
Where are they going (to)?	Kien ili iras?
To a restaurant to eat.	Al restoracio por manĝi.

Where is there a good hotel?	Kie bona hotelo troviĝas?
Where is there a good restaurant?	Kie bona restoracio troviĝas?
Where is the soccer field?	Kie troviĝas la futbalejo?
Where is the train station?	Kie troviĝas la stacidomo?
Where are my suitcases?	Kie estas miaj valizoj?
Where is there (potable) water?	Kie troviĝas (trink)akvo?
There is water in the well.	Estas akvo en la puto.
Bottles of water are sold there.	Boteloj da akvo vendiĝas tie. / Oni vendas botelojn da akvo tie.
Where are you from?	De kie vi estas? / El kie vi estas?
I am from Europe.	Mi estas de Eŭropo.
I am from the United States.	Mi estas de Usono.
I am from England.	Mi estas de Anglio.
Where were you born?	Kie vi naskiĝis?
I was born in New York.	Mi naskiĝis en Novjorko.
Where do you live?	Kie vi loĝas?
I live in the country.	Mi loĝas en la kamparo.
I live in a big city.	Mi loĝas en granda urbo.
Where do they live?	Kie ili loĝas?
They live in Chicago.	Ili loĝas en Ĉikago.
We also live in a city.	Ni ankaŭ loĝas en urbo.
We live in Dallas, in the American state of Texas.	Ni loĝas en Dalaso, en la Usona ŝtato Teksaso.
Where do people speak Esperanto?	Kie oni parolas Esperanton?

They speak Esperanto throughout the whole world.	Oni parolas Esperanton tra la tuta mondo.
We call the Esperanto-speaking world "Esperanto-land."	Ni nomigas la mondon de la Esperanto-parolantoj "Esperantio."
People also speak Esperanto in the United States.	Oni ankaŭ parolas Esperanton en Usono.
Really? Where?	Ĉu vere? Kie?
There are Esperanto groups in many states.	Estas Esperanto-asocioj en multaj ŝtatoj.
The Central Office of the Esperanto League for North America is in California.	La Centra Oficejo de ELNA estas en Kalifornio.
Wow!	Mirinda afero!
And there is a very active group in New York.	Kaj estas tre aktiva asocio en Novjorko.
In New York state or New York city?	Ĉu en la ŝtato de Novjorko, aŭ ĉu en la urbo?
Listen! "Novjorko" means the city; "Novjorkio" means the state.	Atentu! "Novjorko" signifas la urbon; "Novjorkio" signifas la ŝtaton.
The suffix "-io" means "land."	La sufikso "-io" signifas "landon."

WHEN?
Kiam?

then, at that time	tiam
never	neniam
sometime	iam
always	ĉiam
When shall we have dinner?	Kiam ni vespermanĝu?
When is the celebration?	Kiam la festo okazos?
When will the train leave?	Kiam la trajno forveturos?
When will the bus arrive?	Kiam la aŭtobuso alvenos?
When do the stores close?	Kiam la butikoj fermiĝas?
When will the stores close today?	Kiam la butikoj fermiĝas hodiaŭ?
When will the museum open?	Kiam la muzeo malfermiĝos?
When does water freeze?	Kiam la akvo glaciiĝas?
It freezes at O degrees.	Ĝi glaciiĝas je la grado nulo.
When is the market day here?	Kiam estas la vendotago ĉi tie?
When do you like to go for walks?	Kiam plaĉas al vi promeni?
For how long have you been here? (Since when...)	Ekde kiam vi estas ĉi tie?
(Since) just one day.	Ekde nur unu tago.
For how long have you been studying Esperanto?	Ekde kiam vi studas Esperanton?

For several months already.	Ekde pluraj monatoj jam.

Kiam is also used as a connecting word, much the same as the English "when." Its *correlative* word is *tiam*, "at that time." This *tiam* is often omitted.

When the weather is good, (then) I like to go for walks.	Kiam la vetero estas bona, tiam plaĉas al mi promeni.
When will Peter return home?	Kiam Petro revenos hejmen?
He will come home when he has no money left!	Li revenos hejmen, kiam ne restos al li mono!
When will you come?	Kiam vi venos?
I will come when I am ready.	Mi venos, kiam mi estos preta.
When will you all come?	Kiam vi ĉiuj venos?
We will come when we are ready.	Ni venos, kiam ni estos pretaj.

WHAT KIND OF?
Kia? (plural: *kiaj*)

that kind of	tia
this kind of	tia ĉi / ĉi tia
no kind of	nenia
some kind of	ia
every kind of	ĉia
What kind of man is he?	Kia viro li estas?
He is generous.	Li estas malavara.
He is miserly.	Li estas avara.
What kind of woman is she?	Kia virino ŝi estas?
She is goodhearted.	Ŝi estas bonkora.
What kind of town is that?	Kia vilaĝo estas tiu?
That is a small, but interesting town.	Tiu estas malgranda, sed interesa vilaĝo.
What kind of cup is this?	Kia taso estas ĉi tiu?
It is a new cup.	Ĝi estas nova taso.
What kind of cups are those?	Kiaj tasoj estas tiuj?
Those are china cups.	Tiuj estas porcelanaj tasoj.
What kind of chair is this?	Kia seĝo estas ĉi tiu?
This is an old chair.	Ĉi tiu estas malnova seĝo.
What's it like?	Kia ĝi estas?
It's big.	Ĝi estas granda
What are they like?	Kiaj ili estas?
They are small.	Ili estas malgrandaj.
It's small.	Ĝi estas malgranda.
It's long.	Ĝi estas longa.

WHAT KIND OF?

It's short.	Ĝi estas mallonga.
It's good, very good, really.	Ĝi estas bona, eĉ tre bona.
It's heavy.	Ĝi estas peza.
It's lightweight.	Ĝi estas malpeza.
It's expensive.	Ĝi estas multekosta.
In fact, it's too expensive.	Fakte, ĝi estas tro multekosta.
It's attractively priced.	Ĝi estas bonpreza.
It's round.	Ĝi estas ronda.
It's square.	Ĝi estas kvadrata.
It's rectangular.	Ĝi estas ortangula.
What's the tower like?	Kia estas la turo?
It's tall and old.	Ĝi estas alta kaj malnova.
What's the church like?	Kia estas la preĝejo?
It's medieval.	Ĝi estas mezepoka.
What are the mosques like?	Kiaj estas la moskeoj?
They are beautiful.	Ili estas belaj.
What's the water like?	Kia estas la akvo?
It's really cold!	Malvarmega ĝi estas!

HOW?
Kiel?

in that way, thus	tiel
in this way, so	tiel ĉi / ĉi tiel
in no way, nohow	neniel
in some way, somehow	iel
in every way	ĉiel
How shall I go to London?	Kiel mi veturu al Londono?
Take a bus.	Prenu aŭtobuson.
Take a train.	Prenu trajnon.
How shall I travel to Dallas most easily?	Kiel mi plejfacile vojaĝu al Dalaso?
Go to the station and take a train.	Iru al la stacidomo kaj prenu trajnon.
Ride out to the airport and take a plane.	Veturu al la aeroporto kaj prenu avion.

Note: Some Esperantists will prefer *flughaveno* ("flight-harbor") to *aeroporto*, and *aviadilo* ("instrument for aviation") to *avio*. You may even hear *flugmaŝino* ("flying machine") for "airplane"!

How (well) do you speak Esperanto?	Kiel (bone) vi parolas Esperanton?
I only speak it slowly.	Mi nur malrapide parolas ĝin.
I speak it a bit.	Mi parolas ĝin iomete.
How does the train travel from here to Canada?	Kiel la trajno veturas ekde ĉi tie ĝis Kanado?
It travels through New York state.	Ĝi veturas tra Novjorkio.

How shall I send a telegram?

Kiel mi sendu telegramon?

Just go to the post office.

Iru do al la poŝtoficejo!

HOW FAR (AWAY)?
Kiom longe (for)?

How far away is the town?

Kiom longe (for) estas la vilaĝo?

About three kilometers.

Proksimume tri kilometrojn.

How far is Orlando?

Kiom longe (for) estas Orlando?

About fifty kilometers.

Proksimume kvindek kilometrojn.

How far is Hartford from here?

Kiom longe (for) estas Hartfordo de ĉi tie?

There remain about two kilometers until the city.

Restas proksimume du kilometroj ĝis la urbo.

How far is Chicago from New York?

Kiom longe estas Ĉikago de Novjorko?

By car, the distance is not great.

Per aŭto, la distanco ne estas granda.

How long will you be staying in Paris?

Kiom longe vi restos en Parizo?

I'll stay there for two weeks.

Mi restos tie dum du semajnoj.

WHY?
Kial?

Because, for that reason	ĉar, tial
for no reason	nenial
for some reason	ial
for every reason	ĉial
Why are you learning Esperanto?	Kial vi lernas Esperanton?
Because the language interests me.	Ĉar la lingvo interesas min.
I am learning Esperanto because it is useful in many countries.	Mi lernas Esperanton, ĉar ĝi estas utila en multaj landoj.
Why were you afraid?	Kial vi timis?
I was afraid because you were driving the car too fast!	Mi timis, ĉar vi stiris la aŭton tro rapide!
Why did you call me?	Kial vi vokis min?
I called you because I saw a mouse.	Mi vokis vin, ĉar muson mi vidis.
Why didn't you give her the newspaper?	Kial vi ne donis al ŝi la ĵurnalon?
Because I haven't read through it yet.	Ĉar mi ankoraŭ ne finlegis ĝin.

Note: Legis means "read" in the past. By adding the root of the verb *fin-* ("to finish"), we get the meaning of "finished reading, read through": *finlegis*. Similarly, "drink (all) up" could be said as *fintrinki.*

Why did she give them money?	Kial ŝi donis al ili monon?

She gave them money because they worked well.

Ŝi donis al ili monon ĉar ili bone laboris.

Why isn't he opening the door?

Kial li ne malfermas la pordon?

He isn't opening the door because he doesn't have the key.

Li ne malfermas la pordon ĉar li ne havas la ŝlosilon.

Why aren't you saying anything?

Kial vi nenion diras?

I'm not saying anything because I don't speak Esperanto very well.

Mi nenion diras ĉar mi ne parolas tre bone Esperanton.

Why won't they come to visit us?

Kial ili ne venos viziti nin?

They won't come because they won't have time off before the summer.

Ili ne venos, ĉar ili ne havos libertempon antaŭ la somero.

Why did you arrive late?

Kial vi alvenis malfrue?

An early arrival was to be preferred.

Frua alveno estis preferinda.

I arrived late because I got lost.

Mi alvenis malfrue ĉar mi perdiĝis.

Why aren't they eating?

Kial ili ne manĝas?

They aren't eating because they aren't hungry.

Ili ne manĝas ĉar ili ne havas malsaton.

BASIC NUMBERS
Bazaj Numbroj

Esperanto numbers are *easy*. First learn the numbers from 1 to 10.

1	unu	("OO-noo")	6	ses	("sehss")
2	du	("doo")	7	sep	("sehp")
3	tri	("tree")	8	ok	("oak")
4	kvar	("kvahr")	9	naŭ	("now")
5	kvin	("kveen")	10	dek	("dehk")

Note: The word for "zero" is *nul* ("nool").

Now combine the numbers 1–9 with 10 to form the teens.

11	dek unu		16	dek ses
12	dek du		17	dek sep
13	dek tri		18	dek ok
14	dek kvar		19	dek naŭ
15	dek kvin			

For the numbers 20 through 90, use 10 ("dek") suffixed to the numbers 2–9:

20	dudek		60	sesdek
30	tridek		70	sepdek
40	kvardek		80	okdek
50	kvindek		90	naŭdek

Intermediate numbers are simply combinations of the tens ("dudek, tridek") with the numbers 1–9:

21	dudek unu		65	sesdek kvin
32	tridek du		76	sepdek ses

| 43 | kvardek tri | 87 | okdek sep |
| 54 | kvindek kvar | 98 | naŭdek ok |

After *naŭdek naŭ* (99), the next number is *cent* (100), "tsent."

125	cent dudek kvin	580	kvincent okdek
197	cent naŭdek sep	671	sescent sepdek unu
200	ducent	795	sepcent naŭdek kvin
250	ducent kvindek	804	okcent kvar
300	tricent	921	naŭcent dudek unu
444	kvarcent kvardek kvar	999	naŭcent naŭdek naŭ

For "thousand," the word is *mil*.

| 1 000 | mil |
| 2 500 | du mil kvincent |

Note: The word *cent* ("hundred") is suffixed to a number from 1–9. The word *mil* ("thousand") is written as a separate word.

3 760	tri mil sepcent sesdek
45 000	kvardek kvin mil
100 000	cent mil
857 651	okcent kvindek sep mil sescent kvindek unu

Words for larger numbers are nouns: *miliono* ("million") and *miliardo* ("billion"). These use *unu* for "one million, one billion": *unu miliono, unu miliardo*. They also have plural forms:

| 2 000 000 | du milionoj |
| 56 000 000 | kvindek ses milionoj |

8 000 000 000   ok miliardoj

Note: The use of commas and periods with numbers varies from country to country. In general, Esperanto uses a space (or a period) between millions, thousands and hundreds: 35 000 (or 35.000). For decimals, Esperanto uses a comma: 3,25 (*tri komo dudek kvin*).

Fractions use the suffix *-on(o)* added to the basic numbers:

½	duono
⅓	triono
¼	kvarono
¾	tri kvaronoj
¹³⁄₃₂	dek-tri tridek-duonoj

Ordinal numbers add the adjective suffix to the basic number:

first	unua	sixth	sesa
second	dua	seventh	sepa
third	tria	eighth	oka
fourth	kvara	ninth	naŭa
fifth	kvina	tenth	deka

These numbers function as adjectives, and so have plural and direct object forms:

the first three days	la unuaj tri tagoj
the twelfth person	la dekdua persono
I know the ninth song.	Mi scias la naŭan kanton.
the eighth man	la oka sinjoro
the sixth woman	la sesa sinjorino

BASIC NUMBERS

Here are some more phrases with numbers:

twenty-three cats	dudek tri katoj
forty-five chairs	kvardek kvin seĝoj
fifty-one fish	kvindek unu fiŝoj
sixty-three apples	sesdek tri pomoj
I bought fifteen apples.	Mi aĉetis dek kvin pomojn.
There are twenty small books in my bag.	Estas dudek malgrandaj libroj en mia sako.
dollar, dollars	dolaro, dolaroj
$89	okdek naŭ dolaroj
$98	naŭdek ok dolaroj
cent	cendo ("TSEHN-doh")
How much does this book cost?	Kiom kostas ĉi tiu libro?
It costs $12.98	Ĝi kostas dek du dolarojn, naŭdek ok cendojn.
about one hundred	proksimume cent
more than one hundred	pli multe ol cent
almost one hundred	preskaŭ cent

HOW MUCH? HOW MANY?
Kiom?

that much	tiom
no amount, none	neniom
some amount, some	iom
every amount	ĉiom
How much is a room for one night?	Kiom kostas unu ĉambro por unu nokto?
How much is that in U.S. dollars?	Kiom tio estas en usonaj dolaroj?
How much did you pay for that?	Kiom vi pagis por tio?
How many flowers did you buy?	Kiom da floroj vi aĉetis?
How old is he?	Kiomjara li estas? / Kiom aĝa li estas? / Kiom li aĝas?
He is thirty.	Li estas tridekjara. / Li aĝas tridek jarojn.
How old are you?	Kiomjara vi estos? / Kiom aĝa vi estas? / Kiom vi aĝas?
I am forty-five.	Mi estos kvardekkvinjara.
Are you really an eighteen-year-old girl?	Ĉu vi estas vere dekokjarulino? (dek-ok-jar-ul-in-o)
How much milk is left?	Kiom da lakto restas?
How many fingers are on one hand?	Kiom da fingroj estas je unu mano?
How many glasses are in the cupboard?	Kiom da glasoj estas en la ŝranko?
How many people are around the table?	Kiom da personoj estas ĉirkaŭ la tablo?
Many.	Multaj.
Few.	Malmultaj.

There are many people in the house.	Estas multaj personoj en la domo.
There are not many people in the house.	Ne estas multaj personoj en la domo.
There are few people in the house.	Estas malmultaj personoj en la domo.
No one is in the house.	Neniu estas en la domo.
How many people do you know in Rotterdam?	Kiom da personoj vi konas en Roterdamo?
No one.	Neniu.
I don't know anyone.	Mi konas neniun.
How many children do you have?	Kiom da infanoj vi havas?
We have two children.	Ni havas du infanojn.
How many months are in one year?	Kiom da monatoj estas en unu jaro?
There are twelve months.	Estas dek du monatoj.
How many days are in one week?	Kiom da tagoj estas en unu semajno?
There are seven days.	Estas sep tagoj.
For how many days were you in Montreal?	Dum kiom da tagoj vi estis en Montrealo?
I was only there for five days.	Dum nur kvin tagoj mi estis tie.
How many fish did Peter catch?	Kiom da fiŝoj Petro kaptis?
He caught four or five fish.	Li kaptis kvar aŭ kvin fiŝojn.

TIME
La Horo

one hour, for one hour	unu horo, unu horon
two hours, for two hours	du horoj, du horojn
a minute	minuto
a second	sekundo
a clock	horloĝo
a wristwatch ("arm-clock")	brakhorloĝo
What time is it?	Kioma horo estas?
It's six o'clock.	Estas la sesa.

Note: The Esperanto expression "What time is it?" uses the word *kiom* ("how much/many") as an adjective with the word *horo* ("hour"). The meaning is something like "How-much-hour is it?" The answer uses the ordinal numbers: *Estas la sesa*, "It's the sixth (hour)."

It's two o'clock.	Estas la dua.
It's already three o'clock.	Estas jam la tria.
It's four o'clock.	Estas la kvara.
We left at two-thirty.	Ni foriris je la dua kaj duono.
We arrived at three-fifteen.	Ni alvenis je la tria kaj kvarono.
It's five after six.	Estas la sesa kaj kvin. / Estas kvin minutoj post la sesa.
It's a quarter after six.	Estas la sesa kaj kvarono. / Estas dek kvin minutoj post la sesa.

It's seven-thirty.	Estas la sepa kaj duono.
It's not eight-thirty yet.	Ne estas ankoraŭ la oka kaj duono.
It's only a quarter after eight.	Estas nur la oka kaj kvarono.
It's twenty of seven.	Estas dudek minutoj antaŭ la sepa.
It's a quarter to nine.	Estas kvarono antaŭ la naŭa.
It's ten to eleven.	Estas dek minutoj antaŭ la dek-unua.
At what time...	Je kioma horo...
At what time is dinner tonight?	Je kioma horo estos la noktomanĝo ĉi-vespere?
At what time does the film begin?	Je kioma horo la filmo komencas?
The film begins at eight-ten.	La filmo komencas je la oka kajdek
dawn, sunrise	la tagiĝo, la sunleviĝo
We will have breakfast at dawn.	Je la tagiĝo ni matenmanĝos.
morning, in the morning	mateno, matene
at six o'clock in the morning	je la sesa matene
noon	la tagmezo
A little after noon we will have lunch.	Iom post la tagmezo ni lunĉos.
At two we'll go for a walk.	Je la dua ni iros promeni.
a quarter to noon	kvarono antaŭ la tagmezo
a little before noon	iom antaŭ la tagmezo
ten after noon	dek minutoj antaŭ la tagmezo

at ten o'clock	je la deka
afternoon	posttagmezo
in the afternoon	posttagmeze
at four in the afternoon	je la kvara posttagmeze
evening, in the evening	vespero, vespere
at six in the evening	je la sesa vespere
At seven-thirty we'll have dinner tonight.	Je la deka ni vespermangos ĉi-vespere.
midnight	noktomezo
a half past midnight	duono post la noktomezo / la noktomezo kaj duono
five minutes after midnight	kvin minutoj post la noktomezo

DAYS, MONTHS, HOLIDAYS

DAYS, MONTHS, HOLIDAYS
Tagoj, Monatoj, Ferioj

Monday, on Monday	lundo, lundon
Tuesday, on Tuesday	mardo, mardon
Wednesday, on Wednesday	merkredo, merkredon
Thursday, on Thursday	ĵaŭdo, ĵaŭdon
Friday, on Friday	vendredo, vendredon
Saturday, on Saturday	sabato, sabaton
Sunday, on Sunday	dimanĉo, dimanĉon
What day is it today?	Kiun tagon ni havas hodiaŭ?
Today is Monday.	Hodiaŭ estas lundo.
It's Monday.	Estas lunde.
She'll be working until Monday.	Ŝi laboros ĝis lundo.
On Monday, she'll leave.	Lundon, ŝi forveturos.
On Mondays, there's a plane to New York.	Lunde, estas avio por Novjorko.
day	tago
night	nokto
week	semajno
weekend	semajnfino
month	monato
season	sezono
year	jaro
decade	jardeko
century	jarcento
millennium	jarmilo
January	januaro
February	februaro
March	marto
April	aprilo
May	majo

June	junio
July	julio
August	aŭgusto
September	septembro
October	oktobro
November	novembro
December	decembro
(on) the first of May	la unuan de majo
(on) the second of November	la duan de novembro
(on) the third of July	la trian de julio
(on) the seventeenth of March	la dek-sepan de marto
What's the date today? hodiaŭ?	Kioman tagon ni havas
It's the fifth of October. oktobro.	Ni havas la kvinan de
What's the date today?	Kia dato estas hodiaŭ?
It's the fifth of October.	Estas la kvina de oktobro.
What month is it?	Kiu monato estas nun?
In what month are we?	En kiu monato ni estas nun?
It's January.	Ni estas en januaro.
During last month we were in New York.	Dum la pasinta monato ni estis en Novjorko.
On the tenth of next month, we'll be in Moscow.	Je la deka de la venonta monato, ni estos en Moskvo.
And on the twentieth, we'll travel to Tokyo.	Kaj je la dudeka, ni veturos al Tokio.
In January the days are short.	En januaro la tagoj estas mallongaj.
But in July the days are long.	Sed en julio la tagoj estas longaj.

On what date will you arrive?	Je kiu dato vi alvenos?
I'll arrive on the sixth.	Mi alvenos la sesan.
Mardi Gras occurs in February.	La Karnavala Mardo okazas en februaro.
today	hodiaŭ
tomorrow	morgaŭ
yesterday	hieraŭ
the day after tomorrow	la postmorgaŭa tago
the day before yesterday	la antaŭhieraŭa tago
the evening before, last night	la antaŭvespero
last year	la pasinta jaro
He retired last year.	Li eksiĝis pasintjare.
next year	la venonta jaro
I'll attend the Congress next year.	Venontjare, mi ĉeestos la Kongreson.
Christmas	Kristnasko, Kristnaska festo
Merry Christmas!	Ĝojan Kristnaskon!
Easter	Pasko
Ramadan	Ramadano
Hanukkah	Ĥanukao
Dipvali / Diwali	Divalio
the Kite Festival	La Kajtofesto
Children's Day	La Infanofesto
Happy New Year!	Feliĉan Novjaron!
holiday	ferio, festotago
anniversary	datreveno
wedding anniversary	geedziĝa datreveno
birthday celebration	naskiĝa datreveno
spring	printempo
summer	somero
autumn	aŭtuno
winter	vintro

WEATHER
La Vetero

good weather	bona vetero
bad weather	malbona vetero
rain	la pluvo
snow	la neĝo
wind	la vento
the sun	la suno
hot, really hot	varma, varmega
cold, really cold	malvarma, malvarmega
hot weather	varma vetero
cold weather	malvarma vetero
The weather is good today.	La vetero estas bona hodiaŭ.
The weather was bad yesterday.	La vetero estis malbona hieraŭ.
The weather will be terribly bad tomorrow.	La vetero estos malbonega morgaŭ.
The weather was good this morning.	La vetero estis bona ĉi-matene.
The weather was very hot last week.	La vetero estis tre varma pasintsemajne. / La vetero estis tre varma dum la pasinta semajno.
Yesterday the weather was wonderful!	Hieraŭ la vetero estis bonega!
Fortunately, the weather will be good tomorrow as well.	Feliĉe la vetero estos bona ankaŭ morgaŭ.
How was the weather yesterday?	Kia estis la vetero hieraŭ?
What's the weather like now?	Kia estas la vetero nun?

What will the weather be like today?	Kia estos la vetero hodiaŭ?
What will the weather be liketomorrow?	Kia estos la vetero morgaŭ
It will be cold.	Estos malvarme.
It will be really cold.	Estos malvarmege.
It's really hot today!	Estas varmege hodiaŭ.
Yesterday the weather was not cold.	Hieraŭ la vetero ne estis malvarma.
In summer it's usually hot.	En somero estas kutime varmege.
The sun shines almost every day.	La suno brilas preskaŭ ciun tagon.
In winter it's often freezing cold.	En vintro estas ofte malvarmege.
It freezes often	Frostas ofte.
Brrr! I'm freezing!	Brr! Mi frostas!
Whew! I'm melting from the heat!	Hu! Mi malfrostas!
In autumn it's windy.	En aŭtuno estas ventoj.
Spring is my favorite season.	La printempo estas mia plej preferata sezono.
In spring it's often beautiful.	En printempo estas bele.
Is the sun shining today?	Ĉu la suno brilas hodiaŭ?
Yes, today will be a sun-filled day.	Jes, hodiaŭ estos sunplena tago.
No, today will not be a sunny day.	Ne, hodiaŭ ne estos sunplena tago.
Is the wind blowing today?	Ĉu la vento blovas hodiaŭ?
Yes, in fact it's very windy now.	Jes, fakte nun estas ventoplene.
Yes, today will be a windy day.	Jes, hodiaŭ estos ventoplena tago.

No, there's no wind today.	Ne, neniu vento blovas hodiaŭ.
It'll be windy soon.	Baldaŭ estos ventoplene.
Will it rain today?	Ĉu pluvos hodiaŭ?
It's raining now.	Pluvas nun.
It was raining a little while ago.	Pluvis antaŭnelonge.
It's sprinkling now.	Pluvetas nun.
It will rain this evening.	Pluvos ĉi-vespere.
It's pouring!	Pluvegas!
Today will be a rainy day.	Hodiaŭ estos pluvotago.
Will it snow tonight?	Ĉu neĝos ĉi-nokte?
Yes, I think it will snow.	Jes, mi kredas, ke neĝos.
Look! It's snowing now!	Rigardu! Neĝas nun!
It's not snowing in the mountains today.	Ne neĝas hodiaŭ en la montaro.
It's not raining in Los Angeles today.	Ne pluvas hodiaŭ en Los-Anĝeleso.
It's not sunny today in Boston.	Ne sunas hodiaŭ en Bostono.
It's sunny today in Florida.	Sunas hodiaŭ en Florido.
It's a bit foggy this morning.	Nebuletas ĉi-matene.
It's actually foggy!	Nebulas pli ĝuste!
It's not raining; it's just sprinkling now.	Ne pluvas, nur pluvetas nun.
a storm	ŝtormo
a snowstorm	neĝoŝtormo
There was a strong storm yesterday.	Estis forta ŝtormo hieraŭ.

thunder	tondro
lightening	fulmo
There was a strong thunderstorm last night.	Estis forta fulmotondro pasintnokte.
clouds	nuboj
Today is a cloudy day.	Hodiaŭ estas nuboplena tago.
It's cloudy today.	Hodiaŭ estas nuboplene.
The clouds seem low.	La nuboj ŝajnas malaltaj.
There's a beautiful cloud!	Jen bela nubo!
the moon	la luno
The moon is shining tonight.	Ĉi-nokte la luno brilas.
a star, the stars	stelo, la steloj
The night is full of stars.	La nokto stelplenas.
Which star is that red one?	Kiu stelo estas tiu ruĝa?
That's not a star.	Tiu ne estas stelo.
UFO	NIFO

Note: **NIFO** stands for *Ne-Identigita Fluganta Objekto*, "not-identified flying object."

Is it a UFO then?	Ĉu tiu estas do NIFO?
No, that's not a UFO!	Ne, tiu ne estas NIFO!
We're not living in Volapukland!	Ni ne loĝas en Volapukio!
That's a planet.	Tiu estas planedo.
That planet is Mars.	Tiu planedo estas Marso.
Which star is that big yellow one?	Kiu stelo estas tiu granda flava?
I have no idea.	Mi tute ne scias.

Ask Dorothy.	Demandu al Dorotea.
She knows a lot about the stars.	Ŝi scias multon pri la steloj.
the sky	la ĉielo
The sky is blue today.	Hodiaŭ la ĉielo estas blua.
The sky is usually blue when the weather is good.	La ĉielo estas kutime blua, kiam la vetero estas bona.
What color is the sky on your home planet?	Kiukolora estas la ĉielo de via denaska planedo?
It's midnight and the stars are bright.	Estas noktomeze kaj la steloj estas brilaj.
rainbow	ĉielarko ("sky-arch")
After the rain, one can often see a rainbow.	Post la pluvo, oni ofte povas vidi ĉielarkon.
A moonbeam is much rarer.	La lun-aŭreolo estas multe pli malofta.
high, low	alta, malalta
It's low tide.	La tajdo estas malalta.
Between France and Britain the weather is often bad.	Inter Francio kaj Britio la vetero estas ofte malbona.
Fortunately, there is now a tunnel under the sea.	Feliĉe, estas nun tunelo sub la maro.
One can travel from one country to the other without worrying about the weather.	Oni povas vojaĝi de unu lando al la alia sen atenti la veteron.
a picnic	pikniko
If the weather is good, let's have a picnic.	Se la vetero estas bona, ni faru piknikon.

the zodiac	la zodiako
a constellation	konstelacio
the Big Dipper (Ursa Major)	La Granda Ursino
the Little Dipper (Ursa Minor)	La Malgranda Ursino
the Pleiades	La Plejado
the constellation of Orion	la konstelacio de Oriono
Time always passes quickly!	La tempo ĉiam pasas rapide!
Yes, too quickly!	Jes, tro rapide, eĉ!

ARRIVAL IN *ESPERANTIO*
Alveno en Esperantio

Speakers of Esperanto do not have their own country. In fact, the usefulness of the language lies in its being used throughout the world. In any case, we may imagine the arrival formalities.

airport	flughaveno, aeroporto
customs	la dogano
Do you have your passport, Sir?	Sinjoro, ĉu vi havas vian pasporton?
Your passport, Sir?	Sinjoro, vian pasporton, mi petas?
Yes, of course. Here's my passport.	Jes, certe. Jen mia pasporto.
And here is my visa.	Kaj jen mia vizo.
How long are you planning to stay in our country?	Kiomlonge vi intencas resti en nia lando?
Two or three weeks.	Du aŭ tri semajnojn.
Will you be staying in the capital?	Ĉu vi restas en la ĉefurbo?
For the most part, yes.	Plejparte, jes.
But I intend to travel to some other cities.	Sed mi intencas veturi al kelkaj aliaj urboj.
Why have you come to our country?	Kial vi voyaĝis al nia lando?
For business reasons.	Pro komercaj aferoj.
Are these your suitcases?	Ĉu tiuj ĉi valizoj estas viaj?
Yes. Those two big ones, and this small one.	Jes. Tiuj du grandaj, kaj tiu ĉi malgranda.
Do you want me to open the suitcases?	Ĉu vi deziras, ke mi malfermu la valizojn?

It's not necessary.

Good. Everything is in order.

You may now enter our country.

How do I get to downtown?

There are taxis and buses in front of the airport.

How can I find a good hotel?

Please go to the Tourist Center.

They will recommend several good hotels there.

How much does it cost to go downtown?

Ne necesas.

Bone. Ĉio en ordo.

Vi nun rajtas eniri nian landon.

Kiel mi veturu al la urbocentro?

Estas taksioj kaj aŭtobusoj antaŭ la aeroporto.

Kiel mi trovu bonan hotelon?

Bonvolu iri al la Turisma Kontoro.

Tie oni rekomendos al vi plurajn bonajn hotelojn.

Kiom kostas por veturi al la urbocentro?

AT THE HOTEL
Ĉe la Hotelo

Good day, Sir. May I help you?	Bonan tagon, Sinjoro. Kiel mi servu vin?
I would like a room.	Mi volus lui ĉambron.
For how many people?	Por kiom da personoj, mi petas?
I am alone.	Mi estas sola.
For two people.	Por du personoj.
For how many nights?	Kaj por kiom da noktoj?
Let's say five nights.	Ni diru por kvin noktoj.
Yes, I have a room.	Do, restas ĉambro.
Unfortunately, I don't have a room.	Malfeliĉe, neniu ĉambro restas al ni.
May I see the room?	Ĉu vi permesas, ke mi vidu la ĉambron?
Yes, this room is fine.	Jes, ĉi tiu ĉambro tute taŭgas.
Unfortunately, this room is too small.	Malfeliĉe, ĉi tiu ĉambro estas tro malgranda.
Do you have a bigger room?	Ĉu vi ne havas pli grandan ĉambron?
The room is dark.	La ĉambro estas malluma.
How much is the room per night?	Kiom kostas la ĉambro ĉiun nokton?
Is there a restaurant in the hotel?	Ĉu estas restoracio en la hotelo?
Does the room rate include breakfast?	Ĉu la ĉambroprezo inkluzivas la matenmanĝon?

TELEPHONE AND MEETINGS
Telefono kaj Kunsidoj

telephone	telefono
to call on the telephone	telefoni
cordless telephone	senŝnura telefono
cell phone	ĉela telefono
answering machine	respondilo
(on the phone) Hello!	Saluton!
(answering machine) Hello! The Nalo family greets you. Please record your message. Thank you and goodbye!	Saluton! Vin salutas la familio Nalo. Bonvolu surbendigi vian mesaĝon. Dankon, kaj ĝis!
My name is Mr. Smith.	Mi nomiĝas Sinjoro Smito.
I have an appointment with the director.	Mi havas rendevuon kun la direktoro.
I am calling for Mr. Nalo.	Mi telefonas al Sinjoro Nalo.
Is he in?	Ĉu li estas tie?
Please tell him that I'll call back tomorrow?	Bonvolu diri al li, ke mi retelefonos morgaŭ.
Could you please tell me when the director will be at the factory?	Ĉu vi bonvolus diri al mi, kiam la direktoro estos ĉe la uzino?
Call me any time!	Bonvolu telefoni al mi iam ajn!

FOOD AND DRINK

AT THE RESTAURANT: FOOD AND DRINK
Ĉe la Restoracio: Manĝaĵoj kaj Trinkaĵoj

I would like a table for two.	Mi dezirus tablon por du personoj.
I would like a table for my colleagues and me.	Mi dezirus tablon por mi kaj miaj kolegoj.
I would prefer a table near the window.	Mi preferus tablon apud la fenestro.
Don't you have a table somewhere else?	Ĉu vi ne havas tablon en a lia loko?
We are too close to the kitchen here.	Ĉi tie ni estas tro proksimaj al la kuirejo.
Where's the restroom, please?	Kie estas la necesejo, mi petas?
Waiter! Come here, please.	Kelnero! Venu ĉi tien, mi petas.
Waiter! The menu, please.	Kelnero! La manĝokarton, mi petas.
Waitress! A bit of water, please.	Kelnerino! Iom da akvo, mi petas.
What specials do you havetoday?	Kiajn specialaĵojn vi havas hodiau?
Which meal do you suggest?	Kiun menuon vi proponas?
What would you suggest?	Kion vi sugestus?
I would like to eat something typical of the region.	Mi dezirus manĝi ion tipa de la regiono.
Please bring me a glass of water.	Bonvolu alporti al mi glason da akvo.
Please bring us water and tea.	Bonvolu alporti al ni akvon kaj teon.

Waiter, I don't have a fork.	Kelnero, mi ne havas forkon.
We need another spoon.	Ni bezonas alian kuleron.
Oh no! My knife fell on the floor.	Ho ve! Mia tranĉilo falis sur la plankon.
Bring me another , knife please.	Alportu al mi alian tranĉilon, mi petas.
Where is my napkin?	Kie estas mia buŝtuko?
Waiter, bring us some napkins, please.	Kelnero, alportu al ni kelkajn buŝtukojn, mi petas.
Do you have a wine list?	Ĉu vi havas vinliston?
Our wine list is short, but the wines are very good.	Nia vinlisto estas mallonga, sed la vinoj estas tre bonaj.
What kinds of appetizers do you have?	Kiajn antaŭmanĝaĵojn vi havas?
We have sardines in mustard, snails in garlic, and assorted small quiches.	Ni havas sardelojn en mustardo, helikokojn en ajlosaŭco, kaj diversajn fromaĝotortetojn.
I would like soup.	Mi dezirus supon.
What kind of soup do you have?	Kian supon vi havas?
We have vegetable soup.	Ni havas legoman supon.
What do you suggest for our main course?	Kion vi sugestas kiel nian ĉefan manĝmeton?
Do you want something for dessert?	Ĉu vi deziras ion kiel deserton?

Yes, of course!	Jes, certe!
What do you suggest for dessert?	Kion vi proponas kiel deserton?
Our ice cream is excellent.	Niaj glaciaĵoj estas bonegaj.
We also have pies and cake.	Ni havas ankaŭ tortojn kaj kukojn.
Our apple pie is delicious.	Nia pomtorto estas bongustega.
Thank you, I don't want dessert.	Dankon, mi ne deziras deserton.
Waiter! Please bring three teas with milk.	Kelnero! Bonvolu alporti tri lakto-teojn, mi petas.
Waitress! I'd like another coffee.	Kelnerino! Mi dezirus alian kafon.
I would like...	Mi dezirus...
wine	vinon
red wine	ruĝan vinon
white wine	blankan vinon
a bottle of wine and four glasses	unu botelon da vino kaj kvar glasojn.
Bring a bottle of red wine, please.	Alportu unu botelon da ruĝa vino, mi petas.
Three bottles of cider, please.	Tri botelojn da cidro, mi petas.
Five bottles of beer, please.	Kvin botelojn da biero, mi petas.
Please bring us three glasses of beer.	Bonvolu alporti al ni tri glasojn da biero.
(cold) milk	(frida) lakto
buttermilk	buterlakto
(cold) water	(frida) akvo
Waiter! The check, please.	Kelnero! La kalkulon, mi petas.
meats	viandoj

Note: If we know the name of the *animal*, we use the suffix *-aĵ-* to refer to the meat.

duck, beef, veal	anasaĵo, bovaĵo, bovidaĵo
venison, goat meat	cervaĵo, kapraĵo
chicken	kokinaĵo (kok-in-aĵ-o)
mutton, lamb	ŝafaĵo, ŝafidaĵo
fish, rabbit, steak	fiŝo, kuniklo, bifsteko
a burger	burgo
hamburger	bovburgo
cheeseburger	fromaĝobovburgo
chicken patty	kokinburgo
I prefer lamb to beef.	Mi preferas ŝafidaĵon al bovaĵo.
Do you want to eat fish or steak?	Ĉu vi deziras manĝi fiŝon au bifstekon?
Neither. I'm a . vegetarian	Nek unu, nek la alian. Mi estas vegetarano.
seafood	marmanĝaĵoj
crab, shrimp	krabo, salikokoj
These shrimp are delicious!	Ĉi tiuj salikokoj estas bongustegaj!
lobster	omaro
Is there lobster on the menu?	Ĉu estas omaro je la manĝokarto?
vegetables	legomoj
asparagus	asparago
(flat) bean	fabo
(green) bean	verda fazeolo
broccoli	brokolo
cabbage	brasiko
cauliflower	florbrasiko
celery	celerio
chick-pea, garbanzo	kikero
carrot	karoto

corn	maizo
cucumber	kukumo
eggplant	melongeno
lettuce	laktuko
mushroom	ŝampinjono
onion	cepo
peas	pizoj
(green) peppers	(verdaj) piproj, kapsikoj
potato	terpomo
potato chips	terpomflokoj
French fries	terpomfingroj
I'll have a burger with French fries.	Mi prenus burgon kun terpomfingroj.
mashed potatoes	terpoma kaĉo
spinach	spinaco
sweet potatoes	batatoj
rice	rizo
tomato	tomato
fruits	fruktoj
apple, red apples	pomo, ruĝaj pomoj
apricot	abrikoto
banana	banano
cherry	ĉerizo
grape	uvo, vinbero
grapefruit	grapfrukto
lemon	citrono
melon	melono
orange	oranĝo
peach	persiko
pear	piro
pineapple	ananaso
plum	pruno
strawberry	frago
I like strawberries.	Fragoj multe plaĉas al mi.
But I don't like pears.	Sed ne plaĉas al mi piroj.

other foods	aliaj manĝaĵoj
spices	spicoj
bread, roll	pano, bulko
buttered bread	buterpano
bagel	kringo
garlic bagel with cream cheese	ajlokringo kun kremfromaĝo
donut (doughnut)	pastoringo
jelly donut with coffee	ĵelepastoringo kun kafo
pizza	pico
pepperoni pizza	kajenkolbasopico, pico kun kajenkolbaso
butter, oil, salt, pepper	butero, oleo, salo, pipro
sauce, vinegar, mustard	saŭco, vinagro, mustardo
mayonnaise, garlic	majonezo, ajlo
cheese	fromaĝo
honey	mielo
cooked cereal	kaĉo
egg, fried egg	ovo, fritita ovo
omelette	omleto
cheese omelette	omleto kun fromaĝo
tomato, onion and sausage omelette	omleto kun tomatoj, cepoj kaj kolbaso
toast	toasto, rostita pano
French toast	ovaĵpano (ov-aĵ-pan-o)
ketchup	keĉupo
hot dog	frankfurto
marshmallow	marŝmalo
pretzel	breco
granola	granolo
salad	salato
salad dressing	salatosaŭco
drinks, beverages	trinkaĵoj
(fruit)juices	(frukto)sukoj
orange juice, apple juice	oranĝosuko, pomosuko

FOOD AND DRINK

coffee, tea, hot chocolate	kafo, teo, varma ĉokolado
milk, iced tea, beer	lakto, glaciteo, biero
Which do you prefer, tea or coffee?	Kiun vi preferas, teon aŭ kafon?
I prefer tea with lemon.	Mi preferas teon kun citrono.
tea with milk	teo kun lakto
coffee with milk	kafo kun lakto
sugar	sukero
Two teas and one coffee, please.	Du teojn kaj unu kafon, mi petas.
Three coffees with milk and sugar, please.	Tri kafojn kun lakto kaj sukero, mi petas.
Is your coffee hot enough?	Ĉu via kafo estas sufiĉe varma
Ow! My tea is too hot!	Aj! Mia teo estas tro varma!
Wait a little, then.	Atendu iomete do.
My tea is cold, and it is without lemon.	Mia teo estas malvarma, kaj ĝi estas sen citrono.
ice cubes	glacikuboj
Are there ice cubes for the lemonade?	Ĉu estas glacikuboj por la limonado?
Do you prefer potatoes or rice?	Ĉu vi preferas terpomojn aŭ rizon?
I prefer rice.	Mi preferas rizon.
Yuck! I hate peas!	Hu! Mi malamas pizojn!
However, I really like spicy food!	Tamen al mi tre plaĉas spicaj manĝaĵoj!
a meal	manĝo, manĝotempo
Come to the table!	Venu al la tablo!
appetizers	antaŭmanĝaĵoj
a fork, forks	forko, forkoj
There are no forks on the table.	Ne estas forkoj sur la tablo.

spoon	kulero
knife	tranĉilo
Bring me a knife, please.	Alportu al mi tranĉilon, mi petas.
Please bring me a spoon and a fork.	Bonvolu alporti al mi kuleron kaj forkon.
chopsticks	manĝobastonoj
cup	taso
a cup of coffee	taso da kafo
a cup of tea	taso da teo
Would you like a cup of coffee?	Ĉu vi dezirus tason da kafo?
Yes, gladly.	Jes, volonte.
saucer	subtaso
Do you have a saucer?	Ĉu vi havas subtason?
(drinking) glass	glaso
a glass of Coca Cola	glaso da Koka-Kolao
plate	plado
bowl	bovlo
a bowl of soup	bovlo da supo
Two bowls of soup, please.	Du bovlojn da supo, mi petas.
napkin	buŝtuko ("mouth-cloth")
tablecloth	tablotuko
white napkins	blankaj buŝtukoj
This napkin is dirty.	Ĉi tiu buŝtuko estas malpura.
Is that napkin clean?	Ĉu tiu buŝtuko estas pura?
No, it's not clean.	Ne, ĝi ne estas pura.
Take this one.	Prenu ĉi tiun.
a piece of	peco da
a piece of fish	peco da fiŝo
some (quantity of)	iom da
some meat	iom da viando

THE FAMILY
La Familio

The vocabulary for family relationships in Esperanto requires half the work of any other language. By using the suffix *-in-* we can create the word for the female members of the family, so we only have to learn half the words!

father, mother	patro, patrino
dad, mom	paĉjo, panjo
My father knows English well.	Mia patro sciregas la anglan.
Does he also speak Esperanto?	Ĉu li parolas ankaŭ Esperanton?
My mother is an engineer.	Mia patrino estas inĝeniero.
grandfather, grandmother	avo, avino
My grandfather lives in Canada.	Mia avo loĝas en Kanado.
son, daughter	filo, filino
Marks's son lives in the United States.	La filo de Marko loĝas en Usono.
Her two daughters are studying in Boston.	Ŝiaj du filinoj studas en Bostono.
brother, sister	frato, fratino
Your sister's name is Ana, isn't it?	La nomo de via fratino estas Ana, ĉu ne?
Yes, you remember her name correctly.	Jes, vi prave memoras ŝian nomon.
grandson, granddaughter	nepo, nepino
His grandsons are students.	Liaj nepoj estas studentoj.

Her granddaughter is ill.	Ŝia nepino malsanas.
uncle, aunt	onklo, onklino
nephew, niece	nevo, nevino
cousin (male), cousin (female)	kuzo, kuzino
Both of my (male) cousins are physicians.	Miaj kuzoj estas ambaŭ kuracistoj.

Note: If we wish to refer to cousins, siblings, grandchildren, etc. of *both* sexes, we use the prefix *ge-*.

my cousins (male and female)	miaj gekuzoj
my siblings	miaj gefratoj
our aunts and uncles	niaj geonkloj
your grandparents	viaj geavoj
their parents	iliaj gepatroj
his grandchildren	liaj genepoj
Mr. and Mrs. Nalo	la gesinjoroj Nalo
husband, wife	edzo, edzino
spouses (husband and wife)	geedzoj
Her husband is looking for work in New York.	Ŝia edzo serĉas laboron en Novjorko.
His wife's name is Louise.	La nomo de lia edzino estas Luiza.

Note: The prefix *bo-* is used to designate in-laws.

father-, mother-in-law	bopatro, bopatrino
parents-in-law	gebopatroj
son-, daughter-in-law	bofilo, bofilino
baby, child	bebo, infano

THE FAMILY

widower, widow	vidvo, vidvino
divorce	eksedziĝo (eks-edz-iĝ-o)
divorced man	eksedziĝinto
divorced woman	eksedziĝintino
relatives	parencoj
Mark is getting married to Ana on Saturday.	Sabaton, Marko edziĝos al Ana. (edz-iĝ-os)
Ana is getting married to Mark on Saturday.	Sabaton, Ana edziniĝos al Marko. (edz-in-iĝ-os)
marriage (the ceremony)	geedziĝo
marriage (the condition)	geedzeco
Are you married, Matthew?	Ĉu vi estas edziĝinta, Mateo?
No, I'm a bachelor	Ne, mi estas fraŭlo.
Yes, I have a wife.	Jes, mi havas edzinon.
Are you married, Susan?	Ĉu vi estas edziniĝinta, Suzana?
No, I'm unmarried.	Ne, mi estas fraŭlino.
Yes, I have a husband.	Jes, mi havas edzon.
Do you have children?	Ĉu vi havas infanojn?
Yes, we have three children.	Jes, ni havas tri infanojn.
Two sons and a daughter.	Du filojn kaj unu filinon.

VEHICLES
Veturiloj

airplane	avio, aviadilo
ambulance	ambulanco
automobile	aŭto, aŭtomobilo
bicycle	biciklo
boat	boato
bus	aŭtobuso
car, vehicle	veturilo
cart	ĉaro
moped	mopedo
motorcycle	motorciklo
sailing ship	velŝipo
ship	ŝipo
shopping cart	puŝĉareto
skis	skioj
sleigh	sledoĉaro
submarine	submarŝipo
subway (train)	subtertrajno, metroo
taxi	taksio
train	trajno
truck	kamiono, ŝarĝaŭto

COMMON OBJECTS

COMMON OBJECTS
Ĉiutagaj Objektoj

atlas	atlaso
backpack	dorsosako
bag, handbag	sako, mansaketo/retikulo
bank card	bankokarto
bar code	strekokodo
basket	korbo
bottle	botelo
book	libro
box	skatolo
broom	balailo (bala-il-o)
bucket	sitelo
candle	kandelo
(bank) check	(bank) ĉeko
clock	horloĝo
corkscrew	korktirilo (kork-tir-il-o)
credit card	kreditkarto, monkarto
debit card	debetkarto
dictionary	vortaro (vort-ar-o)
doll	pupo
drop	guto
elevator	lifto
envelope	koverto
fire	fajro
fireplace	fajrejo
floor	planko
frisbee	flugdisko
(eye)glasses	okulvitroj
glue	gluo
grammar	gramatiko
hammer	martelo
key	ŝlosilo (ŝlos-il-o)
lamp	lampo
letter (to send)	letero

letter (of alphabet)	litero
the light	la lumo
lock	seruro
magazine	gazeto, revuo
map	mapo
match	alumeto
merry-go-round	karuselo
Would you like to ride on the merry-go-round?	Ĉu plaĉus al vi rajdi sur la karuselo?
newspaper	ĵurnalo
I'm reading today's newspaper now.	Mi legas nun la hodiaŭan ĵurnalon.
notebook	notlibro, kajero
package	pako
passport	pasporto
pen	plumo, skribilo
ball-point pen	globkrajono/bulpinta plumo
pencil	krajono
PIN number (for credit card identification)	kontokodo, persona kontokodo, PK ("POH-koh")
pocketknife	poŝtranĉilo
pin	pinglo
postcard	poŝtkarto
radio (the medium)	radiofonio
radio set, receiver	radioricevilo
razor	razilo
rollerblades	sketŝuoj, liniaj sketŝuoj
roller skate	rulŝuo
electric shaver	elektrika razilo
record player	diskoturnilo, elektrofono
compact disc	KD (kompakta disko)
compact disc player	KDa turnilo ("koh-DOH-ah toor-NEE-loh")

COMMON OBJECTS

road	vojo
main road, highway	ŝoseo
Interstate,	aŭtovojo,
expressway	ekspresvojo
rope	ŝnuro
ruler	liniilo
scissors	tondilo
screw	ŝraŭbo
screwdriver	ŝraŭboturnilo
string	ŝnureto
suitcase	valizo
surfboard	surfotabulo
tape (in general)	bendo
tape (as in Scotch tape)	glubendo
tape (audio)	sonbendo
tape (video)	vidbendo
tape recorder	magnetofono
television (the medium)	televizio
television set	televidilo
to watch television	regardi televizion
toy	ludilo (lud-il-o)
trash can	rubujo
tree	arbo
umbrella	pluvombrelo
visa	vizo
wristwatch	brakhorloĝo
ZIP code (postal)	poŝtkodo

ROOMS AND FURNITURE
Ĉambroj kaj Mebloj

room	ĉambro
wall	muro
floor, story	etaĝo
on the fifth floor	je la kvina etaĵo
basement	subetaĝo/subteretaĝo (sub-ter-etaĝ-o)
the floor	planko
Put the cat on the floor.	Metu la katon sur la plankon.
ceiling	plafono
door	pordo
window	fenestro
Is your window closed?	Ĉu via fenestro estas fermita?
No, it's open.	Ne, ĝi estas malfermita.
furniture	mebloj/meblaro
piece of furniture	meblo
bathroom	banĉambro
restroom, W.C.	necesejo
lavatory, powder room	lavejo
toilet (the fixture)	klozeto
toilet paper	klozeta papero
I need toilet paper.	Mi bezonas klozetan paperon.
sanitary napkin	menstrua tuko
bathtub	banujo, kuvo
shower	duŝo
Do you prefer a bath or a shower?	Ĉu vi preferas banon aŭ duŝon?
Yow! The shower water is freezing cold!	Aj! La duŝ-akvo estas malvarmega!
wash basin	lavkuvo

to get washed	lavi sin, laviĝi
Where may I wash up?	Kie mi povas lavi min? / Kie mi povas laviĝi?
Where is the restroom?	Kie troviĝas la necesejo?
Where is the men's room?	Kie estas la necesejo por viroj?
Where is the women's room?	Kie estas la necesejo por virinoj?
bedroom	dormĉambro
bed	lito
to go to bed	enlitiĝi (en-lit-iĝ-i)
to get out of bed	ellitiĝi (el-lit-iĝ-i)
Go to bed!	Enlitiĝu!
Get out of bed!	Ellitiĝu!
full-sized bed	dupersona lito
to sleep	dormi
to nap, doze	dormeti
to sleep soundly, deeply	dormegi
Are you asleep already?	Ĉu vi jam dormas?
I'm not asleep yet.	Mi ankoraŭ ne dormas.
clothes closet, armoire	vestujo
pillow	kuseno
dining room	manĝoĉambro
table	tablo
chair	seĝo
kitchen	kuirejo (kuir-ej-o)
refrigerator	fridujo
stove	forno
microwave	mikroonda forno
cupboard, cabinet	ŝranko
living room	salono
armchair	fotelo, brakseĝo
sofa	sofo

couch	kanapo
bookcase	libroŝranko
study (room)	studejo, kabineto
desk	skribotablo

CLOTHING
La Vestoj

men's clothing	vir-vestoj, vestoj por viroj
women's clothing	virin-vestoj, vestoj por virinoj
belt	zono
blouse	bluzo
The blue blouse is pretty.	La blua bluzo estas beleta.
boot	boto
Whose boots are those?	Kies botoj estas tiuj?
bra	mamzono
cap	ĉapo (brimless), kaskedo (with visor/bill)
(short) coat	jako
(long / heavy) coat	palto, mantelo
dress	robo
an elegant red dress	eleganta ruĝa robo
glove	ganto
I bought a pair of gloves.	Mi aĉetis paron da gantoj.
handkerchief	poŝtuko
I need a white handkerchief.	Blankan poŝtukon mi bezonas.
hat	ĉapelo
In the winter, a hat is often necessary.	Dum la vintro, ĉapelo estas ofte necesa.
jeans	ĝinzo
American jeans are popular throughout the world.	Usonaj ĝinzoj estas popularaj tra la mondo.
pants	pantalono
raincoat	pluvmantelo
scarf	koltuko

I would like a silk scarf for my wife.	Mi dezirus silkan koltukon por mia edzino.
shirt	ĉemizo
How much does that yellow shirt cost, please?	Kiom kostas tiu flava ĉemizo, mi petas?
shoe	ŝuo
a pair of shoes	paro da ŝuoj
skirt	jupo
sneakers	tolŝuoj
sock	ŝtrumpeto
sport coat	sportjako
stocking	ŝtrumpo
tie	kravato
underwear	subvesto
vest	veŝto (Note the "ŝ"!)

ANIMALS
Bestoj

being, creature	estaĵo
sea creature	marestaĵo
bird	birdo
chick	kokido (baby chicken); birdido (baby bird)
chicken	koko (in general)
chickens	gekokoj (both male and female)
crow	korvo
duck	anaso
duckling	anasido
The mother duck goes to the lake every morning with her ducklings.	La anasino iras ĉiun matenon al la lago kun siaj anasidoj.
eagle	aglo
goose	ansero
hawk	akcipitro
hen	kokino (kok-in-o)
This hen lays many eggs.	Ĉi tiu kokino demetas multajn ovojn.
owl	strigo
robin	migra turdo (American bird); rubekolo (European bird)
rooster	virkoko, koko
With its "cock-a-doodle-doo," this rooster wakes the neighbors every morning.	Per siaj "kokorikoj," ĉi tiu virkoko vekas la najbarojn ĉiun matenon.

Maybe it's time to think of rooster stew!	Eble estas bona okazo sugesti virkoko-stufaĵon!
sparrow	pasero
swallow	hirundo
swan	cigno
turkey	meleagro
mammal(s)	mamuloj (mam-ul-o-j)
bat	vesperto
Have you ever tasted bat soup?	Ĉu vi iam gustumis vespertaĵan supon?
Ha! You're surely joking!	Ho! Vi ŝercas certe!
Yes, I guess those wings would be too stringy.	Jes, vi pravas. Ŝajnas al mi, ke tiuj flugiloj estus tro tendoneca.
bear (female bear, cub)	urso (ursino, ursido)
bull	virbovo, taŭro
calf	bovido
cat	kato
cow	bovino
deer	cervo
dog	hundo
My brother has three fine hunting dogs.	Mia frato havas tri bonegajn ĉas-hundojn.
elephant	elefanto
fox	vulpo
billy-goat, nanny-goat	kapro, kaprino
hare	leporo
horse	ĉevalo
lion	leono
mare	ĉevalino
monkey	simio

People say that
monkeys are
the fingers of
the devil.

Oni diras, ke simioj
estas la fingroj
de la diablo.

mouse

muso

Mickey Mouse is
famous everywhere
in the world.

Miki-Muso estas fama
ĉie tra la mondo.

pig — porko

rabbit — kuniklo

rat — rato

seal — foko

sheep — ŝafo

ram, ewe, lamb — virŝafo, ŝafino, ŝafido

squirrel — sciuro ("stsee-OO-roh")

walrus — rosmaro

weasel, ferret — mustelo

whale — baleno

wolf — lupo

Hey, are there still
any wolves in this
forest?

Vidu, ĉu ankoraŭ estas
lupoj en ĉi tiu arbaro?

fish — fiŝo

anchovy — anĉovo

You want anchovies
on your pizza?

Ĉu vi deziras anĉovojn
sur via pico?

cod — moruo

eel — angilo

Eels in vinegar,
now there's
a delicious appetizer!

Vinegro-angilaĵo, jen
vera bongusta antaŭ-
manĝaĵo!

flounder — fleso

halibut — hipogloso

salmon — salmo

shark — ŝarko

trout — truto

insects — insektoj

ant — formiko

Look! A lot of ants are coming toward us! — Vidu! Multaj formikoj marŝas rekte al ni!

butterfly — papilio

One can make pictures with the scales of butterfly wings. — Oni povas krei bildojn per la skvamoj de papilioj.

(house)fly — muŝo (note: "ŝ")

Yuck! Ugly black flies are everywhere! — Hu! Malbelaj nigraj muŝoj estas ĉie!

grasshopper — akrido

Do you know the fable of the ant and the grasshopper? — Ĉu vi konas la fablon pri la formiko kaj la akrido?

ladybird beetle — kokcinelo

locust — lokusto

mosquito — moskito

Are there mosquitoes where you live? — Ĉu ekzistas moskitoj, kie vi loĝas?

roach — blato

I think there are more roaches on earth than stars in the sky. — Mi kredas, ke ekzistas pli multaj blatoj surtere ol steloj surĉiele.

spider (an arachnid) — araneo

Whenever I see a spider web, I look for the spider! — Kiam ajn araneaĵon mi vidas, tiam araneon mi serĉas.

tick — iksodo

Deer ticks contribute to the spread of Lyme disease. — La cervo-iksodoj kontribuas al la disvastigo de la Lyme malsano. ("lajm")

reptiles	reptilioj, rampuloj (*ramp-ul-o*,"one who crawls")
alligator	aligatoro
crocodile	krokodilo
lizard	lacerto
snake	serpento
What kinds of serpents live in your country?	Kiaj serpentoj vivas en via lando?
tortoise, turtle	testudo
How does the fable about the tortoise and the hare end?	Kiel finiĝas la fablo pri la testudo kaj la leporo?
amphibians	amfibioj
frog	rano
tadpole	ranido
toad	bufo
mermaid	marvirino (mar-vir-in-o)
werewolf	lupfantomo

THE BODY
La Korpo

body parts	korpopartoj
abdomen, belly	abdomeno, ventro
ankle	maleolo
Ouch! I've got a twisted ankle!	Aj! Mia maleolo tordiĝis!
arm	brako
right arm, left arm	dekstra brako, maldekstra brako
back	dorso
beak	beko
That bird has a yellow beak.	Tiu birdo havas flavan bekon.
beard	barbo
bearded man	barbulo
My uncle has a long black beard.	Mia onklo havas longan nigran barbon.
blood	sango
"I never drink...wine," the vampire said. "I prefer to drink blood."	"Mi neniam trinkas... vinon," diris la vampiro. "Mi preferas trinki sangon."
blood vessel	angio
bone	osto
The skeleton is made of bones.	La skeleto estas farita de ostoj.
brain	cerbo
brainless fool	sencerbulo
breast	mamo
cheek	vango
"cheeks" (*glutei maximi*)	gluteoj
chest	brusto
chin	mentono
ear	orelo

THE BODY

The cat has two ears.	La kato havas du orelojn.
elbow	kubuto
eye, the two eyes	okulo, la du okuloj
What beautiful eyes you have!	Kiajn belajn okulojn vi havas!
blue eyes	bluaj okuloj
eyebrow	brovo
eyelash	okulharo
eyelid	palpebro
face	vizaĝo
expression on a face	mieno
I know your face, but I don't remember your name.	Vian vizaĝon mi ja konas, sed vian nomon mi ne memoras.
What a cute face!	Kia beleta vizaĝo!
What a sad face!	Kia malĝoja mieno!
finger	fingro
We have five fingers on each hand.	Je ĉiu mano kvin fingrojn ni havas.
fist	pugno
to make a fist	pugnigi la manon
If you want peace, don't make a fist.	Se pacon vi deziras, la manon ne pugnigu.
foot	piedo
right foot	la dekstra piedo
left foot	la maldekstra piedo
Her right foot hurts her.	Ŝia dekstra piedo doloras ŝin.
She hurt her right foot.	Ŝi dolorigis sian dekstran piedon.
a hair	haro
hair (as: a head of hair)	haroj, la hararo
black hair	nigraj haroj, nigra hararo
hand	mano
right hand	la dekstra mano
left hand	la maldekstra mano
a left-handed person	maldekstramanulo

Give me your hand, friend!	Donu al mi vian manon, amiko!
head	kapo
heart	koro
heel	kalkano
kidney	reno
knee	genuo ("geh-NOO-o")
What happened to your knee?	Kio okazis al via genuo?
It's swollen.	Ĝi estas ŝvelita.
leg	kruro
long legs, short legs	longaj kruroj, mallongaj kruroj
lip	lipo
liver	hepato
molar	molaro
mouth	buŝo
The wisest mouth rarely opens.	La plej saĝa buŝo nur malofte malfermiĝas.
mustache	lipharoj
fingernail/toenail	(fingro) ungo, piedungo
nose	nazo
long nose, short nose	longa nazo, mallonga nazo
The nose is above the mouth.	La nazo estas super la buŝo.
If only her nose were a bit shorter, she would have ruled the world. (said of Cleopatra)	Se nur ŝi estus havinta iom pli mallongan nazon ŝi estus reginta la mondon. (dirita pri Kleopatra)
rib	ripo
shoulder	ŝultro
broad shoulders	larĝaj ŝultroj
skin	haŭto
stomach	stomako
tail	vosto

THE BODY

The dog is wagging its tail.	La hundo svingas sian voston.
thumb	polekso
tongue	lango
tooth, teeth	dento, dentoj
I have a toothache.	Dentodoloron mi havas. / Mia dento doloras min.
wrist	pojno
ache, pain	doloro
She has a headache.	Ŝi havas kapodoloron. / Ŝia kapo doloras ŝin.
He has a stomachache.	Lia stomako doloras lin.
Do you have a headache?	Ĉu vi havas kapodoloron? / Ĉu via kapo doloras vin?
No, I don't have a headache.	Ne, mi ne havas kapodoloron. / Ne, mia kapo ne doloras min.
Have you hurt your head?	Ĉu vi dolorigis vian kapon?
ill	malsana
Is he ill?	Ĉu li malsanas? / Ĉu li estas malsana?
Does he have an illness?	Ĉu li havas malsanon?
No, he's only drunk.	Ne, li estas nur ebria.
What's wrong with her?	Kio misas kun ŝi?
Nothing, only stupidity.	Nenio, nur stulteco.
the flu	la gripo
a cold	malvarmumo
Do you have a cold?	Ĉu vi havas malvarmumon?
fever	febro
Do you have a fever?	Ĉu vi havas febron?
Oh, yes, I have a fever, a high one!	Ho jes, febron mi certe havas, kaj altgradan!

COLORS
La Koloroj

color (in general)	koloro
color (artificial, as in paint)	farbo
monochrome, one-colored	unukolora
single-colored flag	unukolora flago
multicolored	bunta, multekolora
multicolored houses	multekoloraj domoj
light (in color)	hela, hel-
dark (in color)	malhela, malhel-
pale	pala
intense color	malpala
black	nigra
black wolf	nigra lupo
blonde	blonda
blonde hair	blondaj haroj
blonde woman	blondaharulino
blue	blua
light blue walls	helbluaj muroj
The sky is blue.	La ĉielo estas blua.
blue-green	blu-verda
the blue bed and the blue chairs	la blua lito kaj la bluaj seĝoj
brown	bruna
brown eggs	brunaj ovoj
brown-haired person	brunharulo
golden	ora, orkolora
gold ring	ora ringo
golden rug	orkolora tapiŝo
green	verda
green eyes	verdaj okuloj
grey	griza
grey hair	grizaj haroj

grey-haired person	grizharulo
orange	oranĝa, oranĝkolora
pink	roza, rozkolora
pink cottages	rozkoloraj dometoj
purple	purpura
red	ruĝa
reddish	ruĝeta
very red	ruĝega
red birds	ruĝaj birdoj
dark red rug	malhelruĝa tapiŝo
silver	arĝenta
white	blanka
white snow, white sheets	blanka neĝo, blankaj littukoj
yellow	flava
yellow banana, yellow flowers	flava banano, flavaj floroj
flag	flago
the Esperanto flag	la Esperanto-flago
The Esperanto flag is green and white.	La Esperanto-flago estas verda kaj blanka.
The flag is green with a white circle.	La flago estas verda, kaj ĝi havas blankan rondon.
In the circle is a five-pointed green star.	Meze de la rondo estas kvin-pinta verda stelo.
The green star is the symbol of hope.	La verda stelo estas la simbolo de la espero.
It is also the symbol of Esperanto.	Ĝi estas ankaŭ la simbolo de Esperanto.
There are Esperantists who proudly wear green-star pins.	Estas Esperantistoj, kiuj fiere surmetas verd-stelajn insignojn.

PEOPLE AND PLACES
Personoj kaj Lokoj

In Esperanto, if you know the verb, the *place* where this action routinely occurs is indicated by adding the suffix *-ej-* ("place for") to the verb root: *baki* ("to bake") > *bakejo* ("bakery"), *vendi* ("to sell") > *vendejo* ("a store"). The suffix *-ej-* may also occur with nouns: *kino* ("movie") > *kinejo* ("movie theater"), *dentistejo* ("dentist's office").

To indicate the person professionally connected with the *-ejo*, we use the suffix *-ist-*: *bakisto, vendisto*. If we want to stress that the person is female, we may add *-in-*: *bakistino, vendistino*.

human being (male or female)	homo
mankind, the human race	la homaro
man, woman	viro, virino
person	persono
guy, dame	ulo, ino
child	infano
children	infanoj, geinfanoj
baby	bebo
boy, girl	knabo, knabino
kids	geknaboj
apartment	apartmento
baker	bakisto
bakery	bakejo
Where is the bakery, please?	Kie troviĝas la bakejo, mi petas?
It's next to the shoe store.	Ĝi troviĝas apud la ŝuvendejo.
bank	banko
banker	bankisto

beauty shop	kosmetikejo
beautician	kosmetikisto, kosmetikistino
bishop	episkopo
bishopric, diocese	episkopejo
bookkeeper	librotenisto, kontisto
bookstore	librovendejo
book seller	librovendisto
Is there a bookstore nearby?	Ĉu librovendejo troviĝas en la proksimaĵo?
butcher	buĉisto, viandisto
butcher shop	viandvendejo, buĉistejo
Hurry! The butcher shop will close soon.	Plirapidiĝu! La viandvendejo baldaŭ fermiĝos.
café, coffee shop	kafejo
castle	kastelo
cathedral	katedralo
cemetery	tombejo
The grave of a famous actress is in this cemetery.	La tombo de fama aktorino troviĝas en tiu ĉi tombejo.
cinema, movie theater	kinejo, kinoteatro
Hey, let's go to the movies this evening.	Vidu, ni iru al kinejo ĉi-vespere.
church	preĝejo
city	urbo
small city, town	urbeto
metropolis	urbego
city hall	urbodomo
city dweller	urbano
customs	dogano
customs officer	doganisto
to go through customs	tradoganiĝi, trapasi la doganon

We must go through customs with our suitcases.	Ni devas tradoganiĝi kun niaj valizoj.
dentist	dentisto
dentist's office	dentistejo
doctor, physician	kuracisto
doctor's office	kuracistejo
I need a doctor who speaks English.	Mi bezonas kuraciston, kiu parolas la anglan.
downtown, in center-city	en la urbocentro
factory	uzino, fabriko
factory worker	uzinisto, laboristo
Many workers used to work in this factory.	Multaj uzinistoj foje laboris en ĉi tiu uzino.
farm	bieno
farmer	bienisto, (ter)kultivisto
For farmers, cotton is a valuable crop.	Por terkultivistoj, la kotono estas valora rikolto.
fisherman	fiŝisto
I will be a fisherman.	Mi estos fiŝisto.
fish market	fiŝvendejo
fish seller	fiŝvendisto
This weekend, let's drive up to the mountains to fish.	Ĉi-semajnfinon, ni veturu al la montoj por fiŝkapti.
friend	amiko
penpal	korespond-amiko
boyfriend, girlfriend	kis-amiko, kis-amikino/ kor-amiko, kor-amikino
art gallery	artgalerio
garage (in a house)	remizo, aŭtejo
garage (repair shop)	garaĝo, aŭtoreparejo

PEOPLE AND PLACES

auto repairman	garaĝisto, reparisto
garden	ĝardeno
gardener	ĝardenisto
In the yard of our house there's a lovely garden.	En la korto de nia domo estas bela ĝardeno.
grocery store	nutrovarejo, manĝaĵvendejo
guide	gvidisto (professional), gvidanto (volunteer, friend)
Where can I find a guide who speaks English?	Kie mi trovu gvidiston, kiu scipovas la anglan?
Most of the guides speak English.	La plejparto de la gvidistoj parolas la anglan.
My penpal will be my guide during my visit to his country.	Mia korespond-amiko estos mia gvidanto dum mia vizito al lia lando.
hospital	hospitalo
hotel	hotelo
hotelkeeper	hotelisto
home	hejmo
at home	hejme
Let's go home!	Ni iru hejmen!
house	domo
mansion	domego
cottage	domete
imam	imamo
laundromat	lavaŭtomatejo
laundry (shop)	lavbutiko
library	biblioteko, librarejo
lighthouse	lumturo ("light-tower")

lighthouse keeper	lumturisto
marketplace	bazaro, vendoplaco
mayor	urbestro
mayor's office	urbestrejo, oficejo de la urbestro
Is the mayor working today in his office?	Ĉu la urbestro laboras hodiaŭ en sia oficejo?
merchant	komercisto
museum	muzeo
Which museum is over there?	Kiu muzeo estas tie?
That's the International Esperanto Museum.	Tiu estas la Internacia Esperanto-Muzeo.
nurse	flegisto, flegistino
palace	palaco
pastor (Protestant)	pastoro
perfume shop	parfumejo
pharmacist	apotekisto
pharmacy	apoteko
plaza, public square	placo
police	la polico
police chief	policestro
policeman, police officer	policisto, policano
police station	policejo
postman, letter carrier	leterportisto (leter-port-ist-o)
post office	poŝtoficejo
post office box	poŝtkesto
priest	sacerdoto
professor	profesoro, profesorino
rabbi	rabeno
restaurant	restoracio
fast-food restaurant	krakmanĝejo, fastfudejo

Could you please recommend a good restaurant to me?	Bonvolu rekomendi al mi bonan restoracion.
restaurateur	restoraciisto
sailor, seaman	maristo
school	lernejo
elementary school	elementa lernejo
middle school	submezklasa lernejo
high school	meza lernejo, liceo
shoe store	ŝuvendejo
shoemaker, shoe repairman	ŝuisto, ŝuflikisto
shop, store	butiko, vendejo
I bought this item in this store yesterday.	Mi aĉetis tiun ĉi aĉon en ĉi tiu butiko hieraŭ.
I would like to return it.	Mi dezirus malaĉeti ĝin.

Note: Here is a good example of the freedom to create terms that Esperanto offers its speakers. If *aĉeti* is "to buy," then *malaĉeti* means the "opposite of buy, to *undo* the action of buying" which is "to return something bought."

shopkeeper	butikisto, vendejisto
store	butiko, vendejo
supermarket	superbazaro
tavern	taverno
tavern keeper	tavernisto
teacher	instruisto, instruistino
My father is a teacher.	Mia patro estas instruisto.
teenager	dekkelkjarulo, adoleskanto
tourist	turisto

During vacation we will be tourists.	Dum la ferioj ni estos turistoj.
train station	stacidomo
watchmaker, watch shop	horloĝisto, horloĝejo
worker	laboristo
workplace	laborejo
yard (lawn)	gazono
(court)yard	korto

LIKES AND DISLIKES
Plaĉoj kaj Neplaĉoj

to appreciate, regard highly	ŝati
to hate, abhor	malŝati
to please	plaĉi
I enjoy music.	Mi ŝatas la muzikon.
They abhor rock-'n'-roll.	Ili malŝatas la rokenrolon.
I like fishing.	La fiŝkaptado plaĉas al mi.
I don't like fishing.	La fiŝkaptado ne plaĉas al mi.
I can't stand fishing.	La fiŝkaptado malplaĉas al mi.
Do you like to...	Ĉu plaĉas al vi...
read?	legi?
play sports?	ludi sportojn?
travel?	vojaĝi?
study languages?	studi lingvojn?
speak with foreigners?	paroli kun alilandanoj?
Do you think that...is interesting?	Ĉu vi opinias, ke...estas interesa?
music	la muziko
tennis	la teniso
history	la historio
Do you think that...are interesting?	Ĉu vi opinias, ke...estas interesaj?
sports	la sportoj
movies	la filmoj
Do you think that the food is tasty?	Ĉu vi opinias ke la manĝaĵo estas bongusta?
Yes, certainly!	Jes, certe!

I really enjoy this kind offood!	Mi tre ŝatas tian manĝaĵon!
What don't you like?	Kio ne plaĉas al vi?
I can't stand sardines!	Ne plaĉas al mi sardeloj!
Do you enjoy sandwiches?	Ĉu vi ŝatas sandviĉojn?
No, to be honest, I really don't enjoy sandwiches.	Ne, vere mi ne ŝatas sandviĉojn.

OBLIGATIONS, DESIRES, ETC.
Devoj, Deziroj, ktp.

obligation	devo
I ought to leave.	Mi devas foriri.
necessity	neceso
I must leave.	Necesas, ke mi foriru.
He should call his father.	Li devas telefoni al lia patro.
He must call his father.	Necesas, ke li telefonu al lia patro.
You mustn't smoke.	Necesas, ke vi ne fumu.
You don't have to smoke.	Ne necesas, ke vi fumu.
You ought to speak to your friend.	Vi devas paroli al via amiko.
I have to study more.	Mi devas studi plimulte.
It is necessary to study the language enthusiastically.	Necesas, ke oni studu la lingvon entuziasme.
prohibition	malpermeso
It's prohibited to swim here.	Estas malpermesate naĝi ĉi tie.
desire	deziro
I want to learn Esperanto.	Mi deziras lerni Esperanton.
I don't want to play tennis.	Mi ne deziras ludi tenison.
I don't want to forget that.	Mi deziras ne forgesi tion.
knowledge	scio
capability	kapablo
ability	povo
possibility	eblo
pleasure, displeasure	plezuro, malplezuro
will, willfulness	volo

to prefer	preferi
I prefer soccer to tennis.	Mi preferas futbalon plimulte ol tenison.
to be able	povi
Can you understand me?	Ĉu vi povas kompreni min?
Can you swim?	Ĉu vi povas naĝi?
without fail	nepre
I won't miss your party!	Mi nepre venos al via festo!
Don't do that!	Nepre ne faru tion!

IMPORTANT SIGNS
Gravaj Signoj

Bus Stop	(Aŭtobusa) Haltejo
Closed	Fermita
Danger!	Danĝeron!
Do Not Enter	Ne Eniru
Do Not Speak Your Native Language!	Ne Krokodilu!
Don't Drink the Water!	Ne Trinku La Akvon!
Elevator	Lifto
Elevator Out of Order	Lifto Nefunkcianta
Entrance	Enirejo
Exit	Elirejo
No Animals	Bestoj Malpermesataj
No Parking	Ne Parku/Parkado Malpermesata
No Smoking	Ne Fumu
No Smoking Please	Bonvolu Ne Fumi
Not An Exit	Ne Eliru
Occupied	Okupita
Open	Malfermita
Please Knock	Bonvolu Frapi
Police	Polico
Potable Water	Trinkebla Akvo
Pull	Tiru/Bonvolu Tiri
Push	Puŝu/Bonvolu Puŝi
Quiet!	Silentu!
Quiet Please	Bonvolu Silenti
Parking	Parkejo
Restrooms	Necesejoj
Swimming Forbidden	Naĝado Malpermesata
Taxi Station	Taksia Haltejo
(Public) Telephone	(Publika) Telefono
Ticket Window, Box Office	Giĉeto

Train Station	Stacidomo
Vacant	Malokupita/Vaka
Warning!	Averton!
Warning! Road Closed!	Averton! Vojo Fermita!
Watch Out!	Atenton!

SAYINGS AND PROVERBS
Popoldiroj kaj Proverboj

Because it is an *international* language, Esperanto draws upon many cultures and civilizations for its wealth of proverbs. Here are a few from far-off lands:

from Arabia:
Lumingo sian bazon ne prilumas.
(A lamp doesn't light up its own base.)

from China:
En puto la rano ne scias pri la oceano.
(The frog in a well doesn't know about the ocean.)

from Korea:
Por kio oni hufferus hundon?
(For what reason would one put horseshoes on a dog?)

There are also classic proverbs collected by Dr. Zamenhof himself. These appear in his work *Proverbaro Esperanta*. Here are a few:

Alian ne mallaŭdu, vin mem ne aplaŭdu.
(Don't condemn another, don't applaud yourself.)

Aliloka ĉielo estas sama ĉielo.
(The sky elsewhere is the same sky.)

Se muso nur unu truon disponas, ĝi baldaŭ la vivon fordonas.
(If a mouse has only one hole, it will soon lose its life.)

Tro rapida edziĝo—porĉiama kateniĝo.
(A too-quick marriage—eternal shackles.)

Some proverbs unique to Esperanto have also been created. Here are two well-known ones:

Esperanto edzperanto.
(Esperanto the marriage-broker.) A considerable
   number of Esperantists have met their
   significant others through using Esperanto.

Mankas klapo en (lia/ŝia) kapo.
(There's a flap missing in his/her head.) This is
   said of people whose judgment and reasoning
   may be suspect.

SALTY LANGUAGE AND SLANG
Maldecaj Vortoj kaj Slangaĵoj

Esperanto may be international, but insults are not. Ethnic groups seem to have their own ideas about what is an insult. Nevertheless, there is enough general agreement among humans that Esperanto terms have developed for the most common examples of salty language on the third planet. As may be expected, most of these have to do with excrement and sex acts. There are also expletives that are parodies of those found in other languages. Some examples of these are:

Aktoj de la Akademio!	Acts of the Academy!
Volapukaĵo!	A piece of Volapük nonsense!
Fundamenta Krestomatio!	Fundamental Anthology!
Malzamenhofaĵo!	A piece of un-Zamenhof nonsense!
Kontraŭfundamentaĵo!	A piece of Anti-Fundamental nonsense!

These references to *Fundamento* refer to Dr. Zamenhof's original rules for Esperanto. Anything that is *kontraŭ-fundamenta* threatens the hypothetical solidarity of the Esperanto-speaking world.

Among those who use Esperanto regulary, certain slang terms have developed. The most famous of these is *krokodili*, "to speak a national language among Esperantists." Offshoots of *krokodili*, still keeping with the crocodilian theme, are *aligatori* and *kajmani*. *Aligatori* means "to speak a national language when only some of your listeners can understand it." *Kajmani* means "to speak a national language which is the native language of no one among your listeners." Here are a few other slang terms:

glue	gluo
to stick to someone like glue	algluiĝi
open/close quotes	cit...malcit
I have doubts about his "illness."	Mi dubas pri lia cit malsano malcit.
very	diable, terure
very good	diable bona, terure bona
to take a coffee break	kafumi
restroom	malrestoracio
without money	netranspagipova (ne-trans-pagi-pov-a)

Note: This term is familiar to many longtime Esperantists since it referred to the inability of Eastern Europeans to pay their dues to the international Esperanto organization because they could not exchange their national currencies into Western funds.

to borrow and not return	pruntеŝteli (*prunti*, "to borrow"; *ŝteli*, "to steal")
a would-be student	studunto (*stud-*, "study"; *-unto*, "one who would, if...")

ESPERANTIO/ESPERANTISTS

TALKING ABOUT *ESPERANTIO* AND THE ESPERANTISTS
Parolante pri Esperantio kaj la Esperantistoj

Esperantio has developed its own international culture, a sort of tolerant common ground where all its diverse speakers may feel comfortable. And these speakers have developed specialized words to talk about their worldwide culture.

abono	a subscription
La Akademio	The Esperanto Academy, charged with overseeing the development of the language
Akademiano	a member of the Academy
aliĝilo	a membership form, sign-up form (*al-iĝ-il-o*)
alilandano	someone from another country (more friendly than *fremdulo*, "foreigner")
alilingvano	someone who speaks a different language
bulteno	an official announcement
delegito	a delegate, for example of the Universal Esperanto Association
Esperante	in Esperanto
Esperantio/Esperantujo/ Esperantolando	three terms for "the Esperanto-speaking world"
Esperantistoj	Esperantists

206 • *Esperanto Dictionary & Phrasebook*

Esperantistaro	the whole worldwide group of Esperantists
Esperanto	the official magazine of the Universal Esperanto Association
estimataj samideanoj	"esteemed fellow-thinkers," a term of address to an Esperantist audience
estraro	the leadership (*estr-*, "leader"; *-aro*, "collection of")
estrarano	a member of the leadership, an officer
Heroldo de Esperanto	a longtime newspaper independent of the Universal Esperanto Association
Infana Kongreso	Childrens' Congress, runs at the same time as the *Universala Kongreso*
jarlibro	"yearbook," a list of delegates' names and addresses published each year by the Universal Esperanto Association
karavano	"caravan," group flights, especially to Esperanto congresses
komisiito	a commissioner
Koresponda Servo	Correspondence Service, providing penpals to Esperantists

kotizo	dues, what an Esperantist pays to belong to UEA, ELNA or a local group
kulturdomo	"culture-house," a building set aside for an Esperanto library or collection of artifacts
kvinpintulo	"five-point-person," an Esperantist (because the green-star symbol of Esperanto has five points)
libroservo	book service, with a catalog of Esperanto books
membrolisto	list of members
Monato	a monthly newsmagazine
Pasporta Servo	an organization which collects names and addresses of Esperantist who wish to host overnight guests, one of the best travel bargains on the planet
peranto	an agent, especially for Esperanto subscriptions and memberships
postkongreso	activities which take place after the annual *Universala Kongreso*
redakcio	the editors of a publication
respondeculo	the person responsible
samideano	"member of the same idea," i.e. an Esperantist

samideanaro	all those who believe that Esperanto is a logical solution to the world's language difficulties
samlandano	a person from the same country as you
samlingvano	a person who speaks the same language as you
sendokosto	postage costs
tendaro	a camp (*tend-*, "tent"; *-aro*, "collection"), an *Internacia Tendaro* brings young people from various countries together for a common project
Universala Esperanto-Asocio	the Universal Esperanto Association (UEA), with headquarters in Rotterdam, the Netherlands
Universala Kongreso	an annual meeting of Esperantists from all over the world
verdulo	a "green one," i.e., an Esperantist
zamenhofaĵoj	Zamenhof-things, memorabilia, realia, or examples of Zamenhof's use of Esperanto

WORDS FOR SOUNDS AND FEELINGS
Vortoj por Sonoj kaj Sentoj

Like every other language, Esperanto provides its speakers with a full range of *ohs, ouches,* and *ahs.* Here is a sampling of these words.

aha!	ah ha!
aj!	ouch!
ba!	disbelief (bah!)
bam	sound of large bell
baŭ!	woof!
bis, bis!	encore, encore!
brave!	bravo!
bum!	boom! (cannon, drum)
ĉit!	shhh!
ek!	hurry up!
fi!	how depraved!
for!	get away from here!
fu!	whew! (fatigue)
glu-glu	sound of water
haltu!	stop!
he; he ho!	yo!
helpon!	help!
hu!	yuck!
hum	hmmm...
hura!	Hurray!
jen!	Well, there you go!
ĵĵĵ	swish (sound of clothing)
klak, klak!	clap, clap (sound of applause)
kokeriko	cockle-doodle-doo!
kribel-krabel, bum!	sounds of someone taking steps, then falling
miaŭ	meow (cat)

plaŭ	splash
ta-ta-ta	yaddah-yaddah-yaddah
trateratra!	ta-DAH!
ve	oy!
vivu...	long live...
Vivu Esperanto!	Long live Esperanto!
zum	buzz (as of bees)

COUNTRY NAMES
Nomoj de Landoj

According to Esperanto textbooks, if the country is named after its inhabitants (France, Italy, Spain), the name should end in *-ujo* ("container for"): *Francujo, Italujo, Hispanujo*. In recent times, there has been a tendency to replace *-ujo* with the more international-sounding *-io*: *Francio, Italio, Hispanio*. To name a native of these countries, drop the *-ujo/-io* and add just *-o* (*-ino* for women): *Franco (Francino), Italo (Italino), Hispano (Hispanino)*.

If the inhabitants are named for the country (Canada, United States, Brazil), the name should end in *-o*: *Kanado, Usono, Brazilo*. To name an inhabitant of these countries, drop the *-o* and add *-ano* (*-anino* for women): *Kanadano (Kanadanino), Usonano (Usonanino), Brazilano (Brazilanino)*.

PERSONAL NAMES
Personaj Nomoj

There are Esperanto versions of most first names common in the West: *Petro, Marko, Elizabeto, Roberto,* and so on. The feminine of these names traditionally adds *-ino*: *Johano* ("John") > *Johanino* ("Joan"). Lately, people have been replacing the *-ino* by *-a*: *Johano* > *Johana*. Of course, if your name is "Joan," and you want to keep that sound, you always have the option of spelling your name using the Esperanto values of the letters: *Ĝono.* For non-Western names, the usual procedure is to transcribe the name using the Esperanto values of the letters.

The name "Catherine" is given in various Esperanto dictionaries as: *Katrino, Katrina, Katerino, Katerina.* Hearing "Katerino," a person born speaking Esperanto (there are some such people) might assume that there is a corresponding masculine name *Katero.* Conversely, Esperanto-speaking parents might well decide to name their daughter *Adamina,* a feminine form of *Adamo*!

ABBREVIATIONS

ABBREVIATIONS
Mallongigoj

All languages use abbreviations, and Esperanto is no exception. Below is a list of common abbreviations you will encounter in Esperanto texts.

atm	*antaŭtagmezo*	A.M.
BEA	*Brita Esperanto-Asocio*	British Esperanto Association
ekz.	*ekzemple*	for example
ELNA	*Esperanto-Ligo por Nord Ameriko*	Esperanto League for North America
E-o	*Esperanto*	Esperanto
F-ino	*Fraŭlino*	Miss
Ges-roj	*Gesinjoroj*	Mr. and Mrs.
ILEI	*Internacia Ligo de Esperanto Instruistoj*	International League of Esperanto Teachers
k	*kaj*	and
k.a.	*kaj aliaj*	et al.
kc	*kaj cetere*	and the rest
ktp	*kaj tiel plu*	and so one
KEA	*Kanada Esperanto-Asocio*	Canadian Esperanto Association
ks	*kaj sekve*	and the following
LKK	*Loka Kongreso-Komitato*	Local Congress Committee
n.b.	*notu bone*	nota bene (n.b.)
p.k.	*poŝtkesto*	P.O. Box
ptm	*posttagmezo*	P.M.

SAT	*Sennacieca Asocio Tutmonda*	Worldwide Nationality-Free Association
S-ro	*sinjoro*	Mr.
S-rino	*sinjorino*	Mrs.
t.e.	*tio estas*	that is; i.e.
TEJO	*Tutmonda Esperantista Junulara Organizo*	Worldwide Esperantist Youth Organization
TTT	*tut-tera teksaĵo*	worldwide web, WWW
UEA	*Universala Esperanto-Asocio*	Universal Esperanto Association
z/d	*zorge de*	c/o

EXPANDING YOUR VOCABULARY
Pliriĉigante Vian Vortotrezuron

ESPERANTO ON THE INTERNET
Esperanto Per La Reto

One of the quickest ways to explore the Esperanto-speaking world is through the Internet. Below we have listed some basic vocabulary and a variety of Internet addresses.

the Internet	la Interreto
the Net	la reto
on the Net	per la reto, perrete
the World-Wide Web (WWW)	la Tut-Tera Teksaĵo (TTT)
newsgroup	afiŝejo, novaĵgrupo
e-mail	retpoŝto, elektronika poŝto
by e-mail	retpoŝte
mailing list	poŝtolisto
computer	komputoro, komputilo
lap-top	surgenua komputoro
IBM-compatible	IBM-kongrua ("ee-bo-mo kohn-GROO-ah")
Windows platform	Vindoza platformo
floppy disk	mola disko
hard drive	la granda memordisko
modem	modemo
fax machine	faksatoro, faksilo
to fax (something)	faksi (ion)
a faxed message	faksaĵo
person sending a fax	faksanto, faksinto
person receiving a fax	faksato, faksito
printer	printatoro

file	dosiero
zip file	pakita dosiero
zipped version	pakita versio
unzipped text	malpakita teksto
program	programo
Web browser	TTT-legprogramo
to download	elŝuti
to install	instali
bit	bito
byte	bajto
hypertext	hiperteksto
CD-ROM	CD-ROMa ("co-do-rom-a")
to click on, select	alklaki
mouse	klakilo, musumo
Using the mouse, click on letter "a."	Uzante la klakilon, alklaku la literon "a."
web site	retpaĝo
home page	hejmpaĝo
internet server	retservo
internet	interreto
by means of the internet	perrete

Connect with the web site of The Esperanto League for North America at: **http: www.esperanto-usa.org** and learn about the movement.

Konektiĝu kun la retpaĝo de la Esperanto-Ligo por Nord-Ameriko ĉe http://www.esperanto-usa.org kaj informiĝu pri la movado.

The easiest way to find Esperanto sites on the Internet is to type "Esperanto" into the search box of a browser such as *Yahoo!* or *Altavista*. You could refine the search by adding "language" or "courses" to "Esperanto." On a recent search, we found the following examples of Esperanto sites:

http://www.esperanto-usa.org (the web page of the Esperanto League for North America)

http://www.idot.aol.com/mld/development/ yiaz0009.html (an Esperanto discussion list with links to many other sites)

http://www.webcom.com/~donh/Esperanto/ correlatives.html (an explanation of the use of words such as *kiu/tiu, kiom/tiom*)

http://www.pse.t.u-tokyo.ac.jp/~muramatu/ esperanto/index.esp.html (the homepage of the Esperanto Club of Tokyo University)

http://www.panix.com/~kalb/enc/e/eo.htm (information about Esperanto in many different languages)

http://www.distrito.com/esperanto/links.htm (descriptions of various Esperanto magazines)

There are also newsgroups dedicated to Esperanto. Two of these are:

alt.uu.lang.esperanto.misc
soc.culture.esperanto

The exciting thing about Esperanto sites is that they are found all over the world, and that knowing Esperanto gives you access to so many different countries.

By the way, if you cannot use the letters with circumflexes (ĉ, ĝ, ĥ, ĵ, ŝ) or ŭ in your e-mails, you have two choices: either write an **h** after the plain consonant (**ch, gh, hh, jh, sh**), or use an **x** (**cx, gx, hx, jx, sx, ux**). The first system was recommended by Dr. Zamenhof himself (for telegrams, not the Net!), but ignores ŭ (just use plain **u**). The second system is recent. Its advantage is that **x** is not an Esperanto letter, and so has no phonetic standing in the alphabet.

IMPORTANT ADDRESSES FOR
CONTACTING *ESPERANTIO*
Gravaj Adresoj de Esperantio

We have listed here the addresses of national Esperanto organizations in the English-speaking world.

1. For the United States:
Esperanto-Ligo por Norda Ameriko (ELNA)
P.O. Box 1129
El Cerrito, CA 94530 (USA)
telephone: 1-800-ESPERANTO
fax:　　　510-653-1468)
e-mail:　　info@esperanto-usa.org
homepage: www.esperanto-usa.org

2. For Canada:
Kanada Esperanto-Asocio
P.O. Box 2159
Sydney, B.C.
Canada V8L 3S6
telephone: (514) 272-0151
e-mail:　　esperanto@sympatico.ca

3. For Great Britain:
Esperanto-Asocio de Britio
Esperanto-Centro
140 Holland Park Avenue
London W11 4UF, England
telephone: (0171) 727-7821
e-mail:　　eab.esperanto@demon.co.uk

4. For Australia:
Aŭstralia Esperanto-Asocio
Esperanto-Domo
143 Lawson Street
Redfern NSW 2016, Australia
telephone:(02) 9698-2729
e-mail: esperant@gco.apana.org.au

5. For New Zealand:
Nov-Zelanda Esperanto-Asocio
P.O. Box 8140
Symonds Street
Auckland 1035
New Zealand
telephone: (9) 579-4767
e-mail: neelam@voyager.co.nz
homepage: www.geocities.com/Athens/Aegean/3520

LEARNING ESPERANTO
Kiel Lerni Esperanton

Through an arrangement with the Esperanto League for North America, readers of this book are entitled to a FREE 10-lesson correspondence course in beginner's level Esperanto. Contact **ELNA** at **P.O. Box 1129, El Cerrito, CA 94530**. Mention this book and request the free course. There is also an e-mail version of this 10-lesson course at: **http://www.iki.fi/pacujo/esperanto/course/**.

The Canadian Esperanto Association offers the same free 10-lesson course. Write to *Libroservo de la Kanada Esperanto-Asocio*, 6358 rue de Bordeaux, Montréal, Québec, Canada H2G 2R8.

You may also decide to purchase an Esperanto textbook. *Beginner's Esperanto* (Hippocrene, 1994) is a good place to start. It contains a thorough presentation of Esperanto grammar, many short readings to build vocabulary, and plentiful hints on acquiring a good pronunciation.

The ELNA book service (also at P.O. Box 1129, El Cerrito, CA 94530) has a catalog listing many Esperanto books in a wide variety of fields.

BIBLIOGRAPHY
Bibliografio

Benson, Peter. *Comprehensive English-Esperanto Dictionary*. The Esperanto League for North America, El Cerrito CA, 1995.

Conroy, J.F. *Beginner's Esperanto*. Hippocrene · Books, New York, 1994.

Corsetti, Renato, et al. *Knedu Min Sinjorino!* La KancerKliniko, Thaumiers, France, 1995.

Kalocscay, K. and G. Waringhien. *Plena Analiza Gramatiko de Esperanto*. Universala Esperanto-Asocio, Rotterdam, The Netherlands, 1980.

Wells, J. C. *Concise Esperanto and English Dictionary*. English Universities Press Ltd., London, 1969.

Zamenhof, L.L. *Proverbaro Esperanta*. La Stafeto/J. Régulo, La Laguna, 1961.

Also by Joseph Conroy ...

BEGINNER'S ESPERANTO

This book presents all the essentials of Esperanto grammar, and covers the basic vocabulary students will need to express their thoughts in the language. *Beginner's Esperanto* is comprised of 15 lessons. Each lessons follows the same format, with review and reading exercises, providing glimpses of the world-wide Esperanto community. Helpful appendices include a list of national and international addresses of Esperanto organizations and sample letters, examples of word-building, and a listing of prepositions and affixes.

342 pages • 5½ x 8½ • $14.95 • ISBN 0-7818-0230-X • W • (51)

Prices subject to change without notice.

To order **Hippocrene Books**, contact your local bookstore, call (718) 454-2366, or write to: Hippocrene Books, 171 Madison Ave. New York, NY 10016. Please enclose check or money order adding $5.00 shipping (UPS) for the first book and $.50 for each additional title.